BACKLASH
PRESS

A pioneering publishing house dedicated to creating intelligent, vivid books.

Established to inform, educate, entertain and provoke.

Journal Three

A Backlash Book
First published 2017
Reprinted 2024

backlashpress.com
ISBN: 9781068697296

Cover Image: Tear Gas in Taksim, Patricia Thornton
Designer: The Scrutineer, Rachael Adams.
Fonts: Baskerville, Bree serif.
Printed and bound by IngramSpark.

All rights reserved. No part of this publication may be reproduced, stored in a retrieval system or transmitted in any form or by any means, electronic, mechanical, photocopying, recording or otherwise, without permission of the copyright holder.

Copyright © Gretchen Heffernan 2015
The moral rights of the contributors have been asserted.

Contents

Patricia Thornton	The Edge Pieces	11
Linda M Crate	breaking these bones	12
Jason Price Everett	Pale Transport	14
Darren Demaree	Franklin Hiram King in Whitewater, Wisconsin	16
	Franklin Hiram King in Berlin, Wisconsin	17
	Franklin Hiram King as a Welter of Facts and Statistics	18
Steven J. Rogers	A Chicago Wedding	19
Gary Beck	In My Lifetime	20
Mike Luz	Manifest	22
Dana Jerman	Altdorfer	23
	Late Last Night	25
Rich Murphy	Lulla for the Lullaby	27
Timothy Hudenburg	Song of the Mountain	29
Brad Evans	bolide	30
	the old man	32
	late night safety test	34
Timothy Hudenburg	we will return at	36
Riley Woods	Polite Evisceration	37
Daniel Harris	Three Sonnets from The Rapture of Eddy Daemon	38
Jason Price Everett	Autocad	40
Mather Schneider	Possibilities Bitten into the Shoulder of 3.a.m.	42
Dana Jerman	The Kinkotologist's Last Eight Bucks	45
Chani Zwibel	A Special Kind of Purgatory	47
Mather Schneider	Happy Smiling People	48
Chani Zwibel	Cashier Life	51
Mather Schneider	Leaving my Ex-Life	53
Jacob Edwards	Sonnet fir Someone, Someday Night	56
Sreedhar Vinnakota	Shield	57
Jacob Edwards	Personal Ad	59
Gary Beck	The Tide of History	62

Gary Beck	Shock and Awe	63
Rich Murphy	Inoculating Intensity	64
Lana Bella	I am the Dirty Brick Back Street	65
Virginia Beards	New Year's Eve 2015. Manchester. Chiaroscuro.	67
Timothy Hudenburg	within travertine, eventually	68
Virginia Beards	Triangularity	69
Subhadip Majumdar	Youth	73
Neil Fulwood	Delivered Unto	75
Rich Murphy	Lifeboat	76
Virginia Beards	Girlhoods	78
Tonya Eberhard	Divination	80
Chani Zwibel	Good Frieday/Passover/Blood Moon	82
Tonya Eberhard	White. Ghosts.	85
Steven J. Rogers	Blood on the Highway	86
Leverett Butts	Vignettes from Emily's Stitches	88
Steven J. Rogers	Bed	92
Mike Luz	The Sorrow	93
	Wretch	94
Edward Manzi	White Marble	95
	Wooden Spoon	96
	From The Abandoned Castle VI	97
Timothy Hudenburg	without	98
Christopher Hopkins	Mera Field	99
Ricky Garni	Purple Car	102
	Some one Stole Anna Pavlova's Slippers	104
Patricia Thornton	Who is Sylvia? What is She?	105
	Now the Hedges Have Gone	107
Peter Dietrich	The Breaking	108
Ajibola Tolase	Dust	110
	Discovering Psalms	111

Natalie Crick	Rose	113
Norman Miller	Ape-Leader	115
	Anthropological Notes on the Lost Tribes Date: 2067	117
	War Child	119
Tom Stevens	Situation in the Early Stages in the Air and on the Coast	121
David Lohrey	Black and Blue	124
	Beside The Red Barn	127
	Outer Space	128
Julia Rose Lewis	Transcript of the Hieratic	131
	Dear Bear	132
	Hieratic	133
Sarah Kathryn Moore	Validation	134
	Vanishing Point	135
	Vivisection	136
Elizabeth Lasch	Slink	138
	Hail	139
	Sugar	140
Michael Lehman	If the Wild Geese Ever Learned to Read	141
	For a Witch	142
	Shoelaces	143
	Along the Spine	144
	What They Left	146
	To His Dog	147
Rani Drew	Eye to Eye	148
Sergio Ortiz	Postcards	150
	The Martyrdom	152
	The Smell of Sulfur	153
Rose Knapp	Compounded Pronoia	155
	Ἄλφα βῆτα Ὠμέγα	156
	ADavidic CEShrine	157

	Query: [Insert]	159
	Et Filiii Nostra	160
Cornelius Rosewater	Tuesday?	162
	Everyone, Everywhere	164
Joe Grantham	Barefoot Blues	167
Cornelius Rosewater	The Bug	170
Natalie Crick	Rose	173
Claire Scott	Until I Couldn't	175
	My Father: The Little Man	177
	Unbearable	179
C. R. Resetarits	Like Haast's Last	181
L.B. Sedlacek	Physics and Mechanics	183
Sergio Ortiz	Application for Canonization	185
	An Animal Resembling Desire	187
	The Last Threshold	188
Fred LaManna	A Sonnet to the Siren Aksinya	190
	A Sonnet to the Siren Lorathi	191
	A Sonnet to the Siren Davida	192
Alex Hoffman-Ellis	How To Punish A Double Parker	193
	Farmer's Market	195
Richard King Perkins II	Celestial Whip	196
	Gemini Mirror	198
	Gelatin Plateaus	200
Caitlin Thomson	The Yard	202
Norman Klein	White	203
	Reality Times 3	204

Editor: Gret Heffernan

A poetry collection to be read as a continuous story inside a communal narrative.

Patricia Thornton

The Edge Pieces

We were the edge pieces,
the ones with one straight edge, the ones
You look for when assembling the whole picture.
You need them to hold everything together.
The Scary Man in the new house his bare neck
and chest hair visible under this gabardine mac.
Robert Stokes whose dad had committed suicide
ended it all before Robert was even six.
Connie Bedford with her Fraulein blonde plaits
wound around her head, coping,
though her English husband was dead.
Shot down by accident, the day peace was declared.

We sang to Highland songs on the wind-up gramophone
until the voices slowed, deep and gravelly to a slur.

Linda M Crate

breaking these bones

diving into the depths of me
i break the bones
of the old me
rearrange them so i can breathe
easier,
and then i run my hands across
the still open wound of
you;
i don't know why you still cross my mind
we've burned our bridges
insisted it'd be better if we were strangers
yet you're a ghost in the haunted house
of my mind
a nightmare dancing in and out of view at
every whim—
dancing beneath the obscurity of trees and the deafening
song of the creek babble she begins washing
away at the ache of this bones and this soul
i have never had such a difficult
resurrection
this death was the most painful one because growth
always hurts,
but i surmise when this is all over;
i will be the most beautiful flower i've ever been—
then it truly will be "your loss"

like they have told me
for years.

Jason Price Everett

Pale Transport

I.
the white vehicle

she is bleeding in ways
that nature did not intend

machinations beneath
the peeled skin of a world

bombs in the glove box

her terrible brisance
the midwife of monsters

intensified faces
antiphonal chorus
of detcord and semtex

learn not to ask
what the words are
just pray that you don't make the playlist

and the channels of blood
describe streets of new cities
shout as one living weapon

empty shoes in the footwell

they took her apart
smashing their doll
like thoughtless children
for the north wind to carry
into secret places

this hexogen harvest
of delinquent dollars

and storms out of nowhere
that elude control

a continent of anger
demanding answers

some
day
inkless whispers fading
behind the light of screens
recording minus playback
never meant to be recovered
we will learn

not to ask

what the words

are

Darren Demaree

Franklin Hiram King in Whitewater, Wisconsin

Born between two stones
& a green patch, Hiram
learned quickly to be

tender to the green he had.
He turned some green into
more green. He gave height

to that green. He gave his
empathy & purpose to that
green. He loved what

he should have loved. There
is no small amount
of genius in that simplicity.

Franklin Hiram King in Berlin, Wisconsin

Once you understand
what to do with the water
you must tell everyone,

a classroom at a time,
what to do with the water.
This is the opposite

of a dance craze. This
is the cutting of a tether.
This is elemental education,

the only kind that can give
us enough of a life that we
have time for creation

to repeat itself in a pleasure-
able fashion. Joy comes
after we understand water.

Franklin Hiram King as a Welter of Facts and Statistics

Three trips
to a triumph,
nobody

second-
guesses
a genius

if he has
the numbers
to gloat

& explain
his genius
to you in

a way
that only he
can grasp.

Steven J. Rogers

A Chicago Wedding

The institution of purpose. Squeezed from the innards of mortalit.
Pooled on the ballroom floor.
White cotton dress. Cufflinks culled from hipster antique stores.
Wafting in the stench of tainted water.
Dusk. Aperitifs replace platitudes. The skyline — rat race cubicle
mazes — creeps across the sandstone patio with the rhythm of the
celestial light.
Winged beasts. Post-urban metaphors. Placid constructs of structured
banal grunts and stuttered words.
The dew nestles on manufactured blossoms. The lake air stifles more
than mechanical hearts. It's time to go inside.
The band knows all the hits. Divine spirits of inebriation thrust under
plastic lights and fake cedar bows. Foot stomps rattle tired chandeliers.
The cacophony of cloven hooves. Palms open to the light. The great
beauty hidden in the rhythm of ceremony.
Tonight we dine on the perception of tranquility. Slithered down our
gullets. Devoured by the juices in our guts.
Ingested by the great beauty.
A bradlebone tree sprouts from the mangled stomach. Lightening
on the dance floor calls in the beasts — the bees and bugs — the
bratwursts and beer. They hover around their God.
Drink the nectar of the bradlebone. Shit the divine. The institution of
purpose.

Gary Beck

In My Lifetime

When I was young
I walked the shores
of oceans, seas.
The water was clear
if I didn't go too deep
and I could see the bottom
as marine life went on,
eating and being eaten.
The sands were clean
when the tides changed
delivering sea shells,
sand crabs, jetsam,
bright green sea weed,
to waiting shorebirds.

I no longer walk the shores,
but from chair of confinement
I see the brown ocean
tainted beyond redemption
by the spigots of oil.
The fish and birds are fewer,
declining faster,
ably assisted by man
covering the shores and seas
with hospital waste, toxins,

other imaginable filth.

I watch the lonely sandpiper
scurry along the sterile sand
yearning for the flock,
the flock that has departed
like many other creatures
that once shared the earth.

Mike Luz

Manifest

Dreams die with you
in space
leave them
acquiescent
victimless
truth is
weight class
a solid lump
each bag
stretched flat
ultimate plastic
mundane engagement,
blunted topics
finally covered. I mean
something; a shove
not nearness
tulips
in a cage
on a bus

Dana Jerman

Altdorfer

Where I find the library in shambles, water damaged sheet music littering the floor everywhere, I stand and pass my hand thru my hair once- slow. Then a few times. The strands that fall dance down softly entwined thru a shaft of light to my feet. It flees, the light, almost desperately in the same instant, giving way to rain.
Off where I had not looked, magnificent sparkling heat lightning manifested a storm all along the afternoon horizon. I hear curious music of droplets on the high roof then. And the sweet muck and rot smell in my nose open and cool beside the new and indifferent flashlight beam.
More drops find a splash in their usual places. Some collect in my hair and on my glasses like dew. Something creaks- wood or a hinge.
The day had quit fully now- as if disgusted by the arrogance of the weather. I looked up at the long jump of the bits of water and remembered riding an elephant in my dreams the night before. My feet are queer shapes that barely belong to me when I look down from one cascade into another. What if I could trick myself into feeling lost, I thought. For at the moment I was not cold, and wished I had a companion with whom to play that kind of delirious game. And thunder sounded then, like a lullaby as I reached the portico and the deep archway where there was good shelter. I turned up the chair with a crooked leg for a seat, and sat, and had a moment where I played with my breath. I exhaled slowly with my mouth wide open to make a smoke-like cloud, like steam rising from a plate of hot food.

Thunder again and closer. I stared off into a gust that shook the trees in their line beyond the door. It was good then to have the gift of memory place an old gem into my thinking palm. One from miles and years away when I had a love who had a car. In a late summer at the state beach he makes me drive. He covers my eyes and makes me pull slowly across the hard packed sand into a flock of gulls, sending them up. We took pictures and laughed and ran into the surf in our clothes. We were the most human then we might ever be. Except of course when we were drunk, and with us that happened less often than it should have. I hear myself heave a deep breath between the sounds of the storm. I almost fall off the chair when I relax too much. I notice a book under a board where there wasn't one before. It's out of the wet, so I get it up and dig it out. A midsize volume with a rutilant sun-stained canvas cover. No outstanding label that I can see, but a stamp inside: Ex Libris: My Father.
I never knew him.

Late Last Night

It wasn't a night that belonged to me. I belonged to it, and it used me to a purpose for excess.

But if I hadn't gone out, I wouldn't have looked at him and thought.
Thought about fitting in. About the things we do to show face.

How he takes the trophy of his smile and shows it off to all the wrong people.
But they're just people. No better. No worse. And in the closest proximity.

I look at him and wonder what he lies about. What causes his cheeks to flush.
How deep do the roots of his foolishness go?

Perhaps the heart is so very beautiful because it makes no sense.
The blank slate consciousness grows dimmer
under the growling scrawl of other souls you must follow.

For without them
you would be nothing.

I stumble home in the winter air and vomit in an alley shaped like a dream.
I have no arm to take. The world swooning like a dance thru tears.

We are both of us proof
that no one is ever too young
to fall into the supreme exile
of loneliness.

Rich Murphy

Lullaby for the Lullaby

And people flock around the poet and say: 'Sing again soon' – that is, 'May new sufferings torment your soul but your lips be fashioned as before, for the cry would only frighten us, but the music, that is blissful.' –Kierkegaard

For marketing campaigns,
mantra poets calm
before, during, and after
wallets empty and worse.
Sorry Mr. Ginsberg, the mystic
squeeze box vortex fits well
between yawning sex and violence; listen.

Pound pronouncements pounced in Pisa.
Abracadabra Rimbaud disappeared in Africa.
Logy yogi Whitman bought with spirit
"Co-creator of the unintended."
(Maybe, Howl brought to balance Yawp.)

Snuggle up to Om in a new home
not owned for 30 years
but indebted to unknown suffering by others.

Sops for moral outrage
clean up where frames, lures,
and sugar plums entered

into public dreams without inspiring
the appointed behavior.

Should poet pain stop managing
at the life-long hospice,
having to pick rose petals from over eyeballs
could cease and the pencil behind an ear
could catch-up, could win.
The work toward waking
to owning a body may begin.
No one with a breath escapes.

Pluck at the feathers from the song
to expose the right questions
for the birds in the trees
for the dying generation.

The war may be lost
but integrity engages in struggle
to breathe through psychology
with places for heads to bump,
with rough ledges for gluteus maximus,
and with cause for the heart.

Hominid preying on hominid
whine on knees before posterity
laying claim to heroism and innocence.

Timothy Hudenburg

Song of the Mountain

conversations
our little voices
compose

echoes recede sharpen forth
what companions sustain
until we thought

the discourse
imperceptible though
compassion ends

returns again
easily follows argument
this deliberate earth

hollower still
how Zarathustra must feel
when no one listens

Brad Evans

bolide

when you came in
undetected

that cold,
February morning

some thought
that the missiles had finally been launched -

that it was the beginning
of the end.

Eyewitness accounts of the Tunguska Event
appear almost identical –

that sputtering light – an already ferocious engagement,
barely enough to turn a driver's head

And while our patchy, underappreciated quilt
slowed you down

to a mere 30,000 km / hr
the effort to bring you to a crawl brought its own consequences:

that sudden, retina-piercing intensity,

easily upstaging the sunlight at dawn,

cctv footage from a range of countries
appearing in almost >> :

shadows mocking time-lapse
playing catchup across main thoroughfares
through various oblasts & provinces

and then the shockwave – of windows being blown in,
of office clerks scurrying under desks for shelter
a falling factory's wall,
a feeling of heat reported,
those muffled staccato sounds much like artillery fire –

360 degrees worth of reverberation
first in the distance and then all around
as you kept proving the limits of our physics
much like Tunguska.

and to think
that you

were
just a baby!

the old man

My journey

he said

will take me to all the places
I once shared.

It was summer...

And looking out the window behind me,
where I worked,

I'd only just thought of how fine the day actually was
before he arrived

and so I helped him
to find

what he was looking for.

There were maps and some guides he needed
before I watched him leave...

he was an old man
like so many,

but this old man

was preparing himself

for a slow, final journey –

A journey to all the places
he had once shared

with her.

late night safety test

they were picking mushrooms
when it went up.

Although the heat
fell off the scales in No.4

the vertical trajectory
did not hold true to Condy's:

heat-tossed fission materials and graphite went stratospheric
with updrafts lasting 9 days.

It was just an accident, really,
following a late night safety test…

They evacuated the city
30 hours later

and sent in a 23 year old fireman,
Vladimir Pravik

along with 27 others
to tackle

a

meltdown

(and who were laid to rest
a short while after).

With wet-lipped pleasure
the media

reported that Pravik
was to be awarded:

"an Order for Courage"

a small star
that looked like gold

from
a distance.

Timothy Hudenburg

we will return at

[an indeterminate hour]

sand splatter patterns of rain
holes form
—
millions of them
what tiny droplets leave behind
waves race upon the canvas
a beach, disappearing sightlines
wild wrath water rages

it's cold outside
down the Fall horizon
shoreline has fallen

[houses shutter
shops close
time left]

Riley Woods

Polite Evisceration

some nooses do not have people
to disease. please do not leave her
& her beautiful axe, splayed statue
of father & his hollow needles. scene:
mattress body, ice box, harmonized
dripping,

head pumped warm

with blue rope. here they reach early,
far past when good boys are sleeping,
& syphon erythrocytes, butterfly rested
in opposite crook. you are 28 days gravity
fed, unformed in glacier-gloved hands,
skin puckering to meet scalpel

kisses—

they revise rivers, dredge abdomens
to a familiar distant

humming.

Daniel Harris

Three Sonnets from The Rapture of Eddy Daemon

Nym 7

How much older is the 7th oldest Earldom of Don
than Eddy's Don de Arris? Seeded jousters snoop
the accelerated race of dead fathers. Where's a raped
annuity to relieve got-heirs-to-carry-his-name? E.D.,
when the seat impudes the surrogate faith reformers,
beats cosmography into the science of the brain—so new
as to pop the pure late glam of the hand. That's
not new, texts the Inviolated Wife, not adjunct says
Wife Havisham of R. Splaton. Breach liti is subject
to the mage. This suit against files of one yucks off:
friends just next-doored, are far less crafted not to be
a seismograph for lip-words caught queering a Son
of Jejune. Jejune's the melek of the messiah's heart
sold in foreclosure. It's a lovey nym, isn't it Eddy?

Antipersonnel 1,200–1,310 ft/s (370–400 m/s)

Eddy "Dysphoria" Daemon is clinically unsound, Freud's
family romance notwithstanding. He sports a cleaved toupee,
horned eczema, and a hacked-off face with scabs. Charm
is lost on him as he monopolizes social settings. His wit,
embossed with a pas-de-deux, admits fingered différance

and obscurity. It's a quaint scatotheological hoax to occupy and emit scented gaiety on his hosts. He's a surly, sly, coy and crude socialite stuck in a mise-en-scène with a hussy named Elizabeta Borderline. It's all applauded rancor, flash mouthed malice and petty duress. His timely suicide steals reincarnation: pile-voltaged, gleam-surged, drab-jacked, dumb-struck in a pit of phosphorescent gods ratifying plots. His funeral is a media event. The Mothers of Satan speak of acetone peroxide, detonating their M57 claymore vests.

Geisha 794

Eddy won't live past a dythic ygnyfycance, hys brain's cycle of romance won't live que when she dyes. Eddy's life won't skee past his delabeled quf. He dehumanizes won't? Here, in/or/mong dyssocyative's ess-than-human simulations to increase a last-ditch effort to appeal a one death sentence of oppeal. Love's ubiquity overreaches as an offed mother of sundials. Eddy contributes to recipes of a hollandaise parasol with white-powder facey rouge lips. Relimit upheaval's meme. Eddy is sexlees. His wyfe lives arsed in her parents all day beyond seam, be.yon/d sum: s-a-m-e, what's? Eddy's a cardinal water trine/trin, a tad past fifty-two, lucky to be lyvely in a geiko fantasy, o-shaku, kabuku, accentuating the nape of the neck, still styrred by rapture's canon of momoware and split peach.

Jason Price Everett

Autocad

daisy chain moebius feltch

die/tomic dirt klar
globbing on the stink eye
mondegreen di/graph
wax in simzonia:

bullshit detector in full effect

mizzy matter
hand/in round the blood bowl
ketchup song in the air sky ear

deviated septa
&a
one dolla holla

gerber baby captain plasma

gonad fisticules
onna
nightatha living ow/rox

decrement the counter
for/a

tiamatic interrupt

| |

doublecross chronophobe
off/kilter apeshit
check tha stats
&
cash out:

an dieu tha rez pubic

where witches dance

one contagion

under guard

in/visible

with lover/tease

& just us

feral

Mather Schneider

Possibilities Bitten into the Shoulder of 3.a.m.

Get born, seek mate, repo-dos, grill wings, melt in front
of miss universe

ball your socks, jack-off, don't weed whack
before 6, act zany

eat neat, look cool, suppose, hop hip
lope, oppose Hitler's roses, lean the way

the wind blows, support, feel sorry, fart
smartly, caramelize onions

choose paper, nix cook's special, send
kids loaded wishes, hate hate

talk right, break clean,
shame the wild, mount the tame

want nothing, have everything,
remember Rome, sift sand, sport baseball

caps, screw rice, buy American,
guffaw at sombreros, say it is

what it is, pinch lice, keep shrinks, plug in

water picks, scrub molars, know nice

smiles open doors
to Roarshack kill-floors, don't duck walk

heart the world, monitor moles
raise pinky, remember mother's

day, vomit quietly
omit pain, shun shit, shut tombs, pound chest

lock bike, don't call
collect, shoot straight, take in

a show, lick ice cream, tap glass once
sit in call-centers, taxi cabs, crap factories, white labs

fornicate for money, help people, pull strings
graph blackness, like Einstein's hair

jot numbers, make jokes, stare discretely, believe
tv, save, retire, wave spatula

get sauced, pretend to be
someone else, snicker, diddle, muddle, doodle

hold on to the holy trinity
of three friends, forget, go quietly

to bed, tread on he who tailspins, fuck
yourself, be forgotten, chew tripe

swallow down the right pipe

make pee pee, don't think

thinking makes death kinky.

Dana Jerman

The Kinkotologist's Last Eight Bucks

Look there – deep into the idiot empire –
where a single savant goes unfed
by choice.

Skip jokes that are gotten
or were never funny.
Gloss small talk not heard and not repeated.

Moreover the opposing extreme
of any ivory tower artifacts of sin.

Here he is!-
Found out by uselessness and pockets
of plastic crap-toy shaped mischiefs.

Stupidity smiles up the corner and howls
out its un-greeting.

Sky-is-falling salutations
eristic as feathers
left unpreened for fashion.

No ladies man clouds his own judgement
with found cigarettes and deliberate
poverty like the Kinkotologist

who arm wrestles with the hours

only to end up spraining his own ass.

Everything he ever is or was
can be found in a store.

Fornicating with dollar-ninety-nine
satisfaction and laundromat arcade
blindness.
Never thinking of his weight
in queen bees.

Chani Zwibel

A Special Kind of Purgatory

This world is so like the other world you cannot know if you are dead or dreaming. From the outside, and from the inside, it looks like a small, organic grocery store. You'll find all the Dr. Bronner's you can carry, arranged in a rainbow, Eucalyptus to Lavender. You'll find organic apples and bananas carefully place to attract the eye of the holistic shopper or the paranoid shopper. Or the clueless shopper. Here in this little building with moldy tiled ceilings and dirty grey and white blocked tile floors, you will find your past lives. It is a kind of purgatory, a kind of non-committal afterlife, so much like the day to day drudgery of waking life you hardly notice.

All the people from your past lives are there. Your brothers, sisters, fathers, mothers, even lovers, greet you in new form as your apathy-bound coworkers. In Life, everyone is on a journey and everyone experiences suffering. In the dim fog of this weird afterlife, this shadow land of the modern world's imagining, are all the same elements that made your lives many thousands of times before.

Don't let it unnerve you too deeply. Play Grocery Store, complete with working checkout, or sit around reading articles on the internet with titles like "Authorities believe Oregon farmer eaten by his hogs" or "Kentucky restaurant shut down after road kill found in kitchen." Stack magazines, stock shelves, and deal with customers usually so stupid you can feel it radiating from them. Draw doodles, write a poem, or absent-mindedly drum on the countertop. It doesn't matter. You are in the dream as the dream is in you and as you are the dream the dream is you.

Mather Schneider

Happy Smiling People

The salamander the size of Godzilla
on the billboard at Alvernon and 22nd
tells me Geico's hiring
while I drive to Trader Joe's for wine
$39.26 a case
it's true you got to put up
with the chatty geek-mafia of employees
the pluckiest hippiest wage-slaves in Sproutstown
they're so freaking happy you'd think they were filming
Hee Haw
but it's worth it.

I get back in my car
9 a.m.
I catch a buzz for a few hours
then go pick up Araceli
at McDonald's.

She emerges crabby as an underpaid baby sitter
from the Ronny World bullshit
tosses a cold Big Mac at me
loosens her blue tie.

Thank God it's Friday, she says.
It's Thursday, I say.

Chingado, she says.

When you gonna find a job? she says.

Trader Joe's is hiring, I say, they need
some "Happy, smiling people."

She snorts
grabs my Big Mac and throws it out the window.

Did you get wine? she says.

Si, Bonita, I say.

You look sexy in your uniform, I say.

Ja! she says

but she's smiling now.

She IS sexy in that uniform
which she tears off at home
before she even reaches the bathroom
tells me to get her a glass of wine
jumps in the shower.

3 minutes later she's singing along
to the Mexican song on the radio
washing French fry crap
out of her long Mexican hair.

The afternoon is young.
A gecko slithers across the windowsill
and disappears
like a subtitle in a movie

gone too fast to read.

Chani Zwibel

Cashier Life
(previously published at The Song Is Mcy 5, 2016)

Dreams used to be more than wishing for a working credit or debit machine.
No negative thoughts, but do not use the word "no".
Just a cashier today, not head cashier or customer service or even a writer; just a cashier.
To scan and bag, to answer phone, to spray citrus cleaner and wipe off dirt.
An old man's fingers,
Long and bony,
His hands are hairy spiders with skinny legs.
To take money and drink water and joke with the guys.
Electric starlight on the cove of nowhere
Blessed edge of forgotten worlds
Find me here, and in dreams.
Circular swing of time
Going round, spinning back in on itself,
Carries me to a place
Where all my past lives converge
And everyone I ever knew
Is there.
Memories live in the wings of music
Vegetables pay us no mind
We are poor vagabonds beside the doors of commerce
Echo me no angel's cry

I can't go back to those old days

The new me is where the old me cannot go
I am time's prisoner.
It's the slips of debit and credit cards held together with a paper clip.
It's the cloying smell of old ladies' perfume.
It's the dull headache at the top of the head.
It's the bump of the shark on the ankle, brief brush with the Dark Agency.
It's the face that haunts, vampire-like, the common place healthfood store that is my purgatory. You know the people from past lives. The same ones who broke you heart with their beauty, the same ones who rushes in every Fall, Autumnal like the dying season, their poignant nostalgia, their cloves and crumpled leaves.
For every thick-headed slow-witted customer, for every Senior who demands their discount, the balances are disrupted with changing weights.
For dollars and cents
For returns and rents.

Mather Schneider

Leaving My Ex-Life

Happy tonight
a tequila bottle bends
like a pencil shaking
in Mayahuel's fingers.

I suck the last lime
of Mazatlan

grimace

then roam to lay the ghost of me
through a sugarless chocolate breeze.

The stars have all lined up
like dominoes
made from the teeth of lost people
and fall flat to sleep
like the clicks of insects that suddenly go quiet
when I walk by.

Happy tonight
pressed into the present
all the words in the world slurred together
like the barking of coyotes at the door.
I open up to let them in—

they bound off like thick-hided fish
in fur jelly.

Happy tonight
set down by a river of gravel
which flows so lazy only the lizards can hear it
the wise old lizards eating ants
like lines of drop candy
on their way to Tumacacori
hill.

Happy tonight
this night of music
numbed by the million opinions floating like laughing gas
that disappears before it reaches my ears, my ears
pinned like two extinct moths to a porous tablet
and I'm freed by the knowledge of my 8 year old self
twisting on a sheet of tin.

The water table sinks and the javelinas crush
their musk into the dry hillsides
this dead happy all-willing soul
where nothing is flat enough
to be true.
I write "HAPPY" into the sand like a blind man
one letter on top of the other
as a scorpion crawls into my ear
scratches an unknown name on my brain
one letter on top of the other.

My soul is dust and ash
the only thing left to burn are my teeth
but I have no match
my torch drowned in its own rapture.

There is a crinkling in my head
like a child opening up a piece of brittle
or beetles eating
each other
but there is no pain except the idea of pain
a hollow rock in the floodplain
that nothing comes out of when broken
and the air smells like creosote in lightning
a rain that evaporates before touching
my face.

They say the leaves of the creosote bush are medicine
but I am not sick

no I am not sick
I am happy
tonight.

I sit on the pebbles of a
smashed self

and I do not want
anything.

Jacob Edwards

Sonnet for Someone, Someday Night

where light forsakes us, life must take a stand
and not be drawn by vacuum's awful pull
besotted of the gloom; nay, fashion plans
instead, you toucans bright, with feathers full
in purple pants and prince-like pulsing grooves
take flight in friendship, flock not false; together
burdens borne turn burdens shed, blown through
to halls adorned with flowers, fruits of plenty
a cornucopia, we hit the road
and honk the horn with joie de vivre; park
and walk and laugh and joke, of seeds spring-sown
the autumn chill receding in our hearts
where light awakens, life must stay inspired
and trill the dawn, the daybreak in her smile

Sreedhar Vinnakota

Shield

Who are these people
who speak of bird-song
and hush you to listen
to the secrets of the dead
leaves rustling under feet?

What of the wind
caressing and smoothing
hills, blowing rain-
drops crackling
off hot roofs?

What are these sounds
they hear of brooks
whispering, and moist
pebbles rounded,
unbeknownst to them?

I'm uncouth, rough-hewed
in perpetual torpor
shielded from song
and sound by layers
of sheer emptiness.

Stop knocking

on it which gives way
to more of the same.

Slashing emptiness with hollow
endearment bleeds emptiness.

Jacob Edwards

Personal Ad

i want true romance
like a two-stanza song from the 80s
in synthpop, a simple advancement of love
upbeat, speechless, the singer retreating
at last in a heartfelt procession
of la-la-la-las

i want to be loved
like a cult classic space opera
kissed beyond mission's end, judged not
my faults turned to virtues beyond ratings
and questionable dress sense
my sets shaking, passionately dated
yet longed for, with each passing decade
our hearts' gravitation grown stronger

i want conversation
like a dr. seuss picture book
simple, exquisite, and vividly painted
in odd swathes, original, each page parading
a peerless assortment of thoughts rhymed
a vibrant exchange between two creatures
caught up, cavorting the halls of a palace
both courting and drawn to the beauty
of each other's imagination

i want to have sex
like an old-fashioned telephone
dialling to the end of a bell curve
then letting the handset purr back into place
(yes, it's fixed, it's a home phone, no roaming
my word, though, the cord gives you flex)
there's no texting, no faceless and faraway
tête-à-tête on the run, never wondering
how great the reception is, how long the battery life
just where you'll be when it chooses to go off
at home there's the race to bring each digit
sequenced, encoded, tender, unique
through a cascading tremble to bell-ringing human
connection

i want to grow old next to you
like the hitchhiker's guide text adventure
my words still surprising, my programming vexing
and better than anything new in a fatuous world
interacting with wit and with charm
at peace with each other, no vogons
just hope in our hearts, every day, every game
when the ravenous bugblatter beast
brings us back to the start

i want to die — if i die — having played
like a freestanding arcade game
at the skateway, larger than life, timeless
with a brightly lit coin return slot
and the option to continue

will you join me? the skaters glide round

mostly sending the hands of time backwards
i hope that you'll be there beside me
to share in this life that i've found

Gary Beck

The Tide of History

Empires rise, fall,
endure a few moments,
leave a shallow mark,
borders on an old map,
a chapter or two
in mildewed book,
recently replaced
by the internet.
Boundaries are remembered
by fewer and fewer
students of the past
comfortably placed
in nests of security
in a university,
where like their raucous kin,
media mouthpieces,
they bray certainty
without responsibility,
without accountability,
one horde telling us faster,
the other telling us louder,
what we did wrong,
what we should have done.

Shock and Awe

Disaster follows disaster
in a once resilient nation
that absorbed all disruptions,
wondered, grieved, recovered, rebuilt.
Now elements of doubt,
a disease of apprehension
pervades our troubled land,
inflicting deprivations
on heirs to prosperity,
completely unprepared
for the struggle for survival.

Rich Murphy

Inoculating Intensity

The path to sincerity choreographed
with punchlines awaits convergent noses.

Guffaws pull out stingers from the blows
that day and night introduce to cheeks.

A week after, the stepping stones,
each punctuated with a gulf on all sides,
tickle with irony and paradox.

A practiced comedic audience
in ballet slippers finesses little
on the feather-planted landing pads.

Lemmings in army boots march off edgy topics.

Every flight and fancy let down contends
with satellites dishes and infinite forks in the road.

Once butted, the cancan foreheads focus
with permission from Sarcasm Anonymous,

getting at, without a smirk,
brass tacks embedded in funny bones.

Lana Bella

I am the Dirty Brick Back Street

I am the dirty brick back street,
the clay tracks vibrating beneath time,
the remnants of this greased lonesome town,
the dark-washed semantics without a proper name—
I remember the big fire of 99'that singed
those slick, blue masonry walls:
the ones still stand as battery for the same
cornered liquor store,
and it is where my eyes always crawl up to the sky
at daybreak—
waking now, I struggle to get ready for the day,
so I nurse my body drinking the gin-soaked puddles
when September heat squeezes sweat and pulses
trickling from the armpits of the city,
with piss and laundry water drag languidly behind,

I am the dirty brick back street,
the subtext of an afterthought with the rushes of
exhausted labor,
of heavy dust-trinket lining my mouth to chest,
of someone always traveling away then coming back,
of snagged roots poking from my insides out,
of oil-leaked motorcars pouring hot tears over my palms,
of rare evenings plucking marionette's strings
from my ill-trodden back,

and each time the wind would come and sweep
away the rich stench and quagmire of rot,
tracing again the ripped cuticles of my street,
while I inner-line my brick underpass
with crimson meals of roadkill—

Virginia Beards

New Year's Eve 2015. Manchester. Chiaroscuro.

A Caravaggio brawl on Well Street –
policeman pins down reveler,
frantic mink coat remonstrates
begs her mate to cooperate,
her red skirt, a bright splotch,
a painter's enduring strategy.
A flat-out sprawler clutches a beer,
a stylish white coat smirks,
at the fleshy gap
between pants and shirt,
at the belly scraping wet pavement.
Law enforcers, a fluorescent yellow presence.

The background a triumph of chiaroscuro –
Black Maria, black jacketed boys, leggy girls
in black minis. Indolent, smoking, flirting, gawking
casually taking-in the curbside drama
the momentary play let of lust and shout
but nothing to write home about.

History glimmers in place and mind –
warehouses, mills, canals and damp
drunks, desperates and loiterers
the knife in the alley, the consumptive's cough
a roman street brawl in Mancunian dress.

Timothy Hudenburg

within travertine, eventually

see the existential self
once Rodin chisels marble away
exposed veins of oxidized silver grey blue
and all I think of is you

draped goddesses demure in their corner
Grecian modesty with no particular order
– another weekend soccer game
I've forgotten the score

somewhere the Dying Gaul
still dies above a polished floor
heroic nudity near pathos now
his perfect Carrara heart almost stone

Jason Price Everett

Plan B

sapropel kerogen
sop to the minor leagues
drop trou / trop drow
& keep rollin sixes

sole rage quit
how to void:

polygon incendiary

make you a believer

nuke the site from orbit

yqy

seven commercials &
not all there

glitter bleach & lava
on to genii recap

short swisher sweet
&
alla prima punkt/zahl

vex/head vermouthës
three minute rule

k/roll king
save image as:

mem/sa strict
& all freed men
are a watch over

spell spell
terminate well

Virginia Beards

Triangularity

Consider the geometry of triangles,

The gymnastics of equilateral, isosceles,

Right triangle and scalene.

Let A = Alice, B = Bob, C = Cathy.

Observe them in the equilateral—

Balanced and tidy, geometrically correct.

Totally fake, shills of abstract concept.

Deploy them to a right triangle.

Flat Alice duly supports upright Bob,

Bob times-out from vertical probity,

Bob glides along the hypotenuse with Cathy,

In a joyous respite from the perpendicular.

An isosceles crisis threatens.

Alice's base shrinks,

Tension builds in all the angles,

Bob and Cathy join at the apex.

That Cathy! slanty, engaging,

A scalene in disguise! a challenge to calculate—

Squatter on the San Andreas fault of domesticity.

Subhadip Majumdar

Youth

That one buttonless shirt of youth
I don't wear it any more
But I keep it near the mirror
In bright sun in faint moon in night of storms
It flashes in the mirror
Naked, I slowly walk to it and touch the shirt
Wear it in the darkness of the room
I feel my age shading off
A little more burning within chest,a sip in coffee
Those young dreams comes back to me spread all over my body
Asking me,how far how far how far
You have made us true?
One for the woman keeps on changing faces
One for the highway never cease to call me
One about those words vanishes in my blood
I know it will be there
I would inherit it someday
The first touches
The first love
The first kiss
All painted on the shirt
I can see it
I smile at them
And I sleep with the shirt on the whole night
In morning in sunlight I see the shirt again kept in a drawer near the

mirror
Silent after a full night of wild dreams.

Neil Fulwood

Delivered Unto

Ground mists engulf its wheels. The trailer
occupies the middle distance in a rough-grass field,
as if satnav led some trucker
off the beaten track — was taken at its word.

Forty feet from faded "long vehicle" sign
to pinion denied any fifth-wheel coupling
since whenever (trailers reckon time
by miles covered, loading and unloading),

it's one of the missing — road haulage
equivalent of lost at sea. Delivery note
slipped through unsigned; logistics
missed it. The container's padlocked,

contents forgotten; useless: rank or rusted,
unfit for purpose. Along the side, GET READY
TO MEET YOUR MAKER painted in neat
stark letters, visible from heaven.

Rich Murphy

Lifeboat

The long steamed habits and rituals
kiss at the bow and stern
and with mythology fasten
length-wise and at ribs.
Without sail, rudder, or oar
marriage lunched when launched.

Calm, waterspouts, and hurricane gale
engage without concern for invention,
ceremony, or flotsam amid currents.
Adrift without spar and soon
without sextant, a compass mock-salutes.

Crest-fallen and heaved, the hull
hollers and gurgles so that
few couples arrive at wherever,
and sometimes one bales against resentment
to harbor for the drowned.

Make believe and half truths
hold for the hold by two.
Boat building team mates
begin with clouds and talk
about fair whether in the drink
or down the sink in a future:

Frantic waves at the passing
once upon a time.

Virginia Beards

Girlhoods

In spangled skirts and push-up bras,
The swirling child-women
Twirl, shake pom-poms, jig,
Prance and shout at cars,
Rattle booster cans.
Celebrants of the football team.
Hand maidens to hormones
and high school heroes.

Slouchy girl smoking on a stairwell
Gets a pom-pom swish in her face,
Her cigarette a near miss.
Deep inhale-exhale soul sigh of life.
Immobile loner encased in skinny jeans,
She gazes at the screaming bacchantes.
Her girlhood shelf-life about to expire.

We excavate from the girlhood strata
Museum quality artifacts:
Storybook dolls, kickball,
Slumber parties, a sneaked cigarette or two,
Cherry Ames and Nancy Drew,

The Bobbsey Twins, The Alcott girls;
Jane Austen's dauntingly chaste heroines.

Archived too in a dusty back room—
The drug-addled mother, promiscuous daughter,

Problematic father. Goneril and Regan.

Tonya Eberhard

Divination

Fragile fall, night comes on so early.
Sets on slow, like ink spreading through water.

November of rotten pumpkins,
obsessive compulsive ritual prayers.

Moving her pottery from kiln
to garage. Thick bowls, decorative leaves of clay.

Tamed wet earth and air, its shape birthed in
dizzying turns by a pumping petal.

Precision, conciseness in creation.
How lovely to think everyone is made this way.

Last bowl lifted by thin arms.
How curious, staring into its endless depths.

Wait—here is what is seen.
Two separate shadows merging into one, bold black

spreading to form a gallows tree.
Tasting a spoonful of stars from a soup ladle.

Then smoke, thunderous crack of a gun.

The last supper splitting into stone halves.

Sheets twisted into ropes of wrinkled skin,
umbilical cord of sleep.

Arms outstretched, beckoning a figure to
dive from a cliff. Jump, I will catch you.

Thin fingers from thin arms startle,
beginning to silently count, tapping the index finger.

A prayer to the patron saint of repetition,
a signing of the cross against all evil.

Chani Zwibel

Good Friday/Passover/Blood Moon

I am going out to my backyard
to have matzo and wine
and stare at the night sky,
with the full moon,
round orb of our closest space rock,
reflecting sunlight in its luminous golden way.
I try as hard as I can,
wherever I go,
to freak out my neighbors as much as possible
until I'm quite sure they think I'm crazy,
which is what I want, so they leave me alone.
I need to be alone to go on this hand-crafted,
stitched-together-from-multiple-traditions journey.
I'm out there having a matzo
and drinking kosher blackberry wine,
hiding a piece of matzo
in the grave of a rock altar,
gazing at the moon,
blessing god and goddess,
and the Christ-god,
Passover lamb,
blood sacrifice.
I am a Christian's child,
and a Jew's child.
Somewhere in there also,

back in the trees,
waits an old Druid.
What do I know of the divine
but Jesus and Moses,
a desert people's spiritual wanderings?
What do I know of the divine,
But moonlight and soft breeze
caught in an ancient oak's branches?
I am a dreamer.
I see both visions pleasant
and visions terrifying.
I've dreamed
of the Adversary
and the Messiah.
Gods and angels are beautiful,
like no human can be.
They have power.
If I have seen such living dreams,
am I not a vessel?
Am I not a part
of the floating fabric,
the dark matter,
binding a physical existence to a spiritual one?
Breathing deeply of the night air,
I promise myself
I can move forward from fear.
I can let go
of those things
that hurt me.
My spirituality becomes

a white tea light candle burning,
throwing sadness and shadows
on rough beams
of a makeshift cross,
scene of suffering,
execution stake,
holy relic,
and ancient tree.

Tonya Eberhard

White. Ghosts.

She wanted to see ghosts. They ran off
after rehearsal to a downtown restaurant.
It was closed, closed and dark. In the cold,
they loitered around like a bunch of bums.
She insisted on seeing ghosts. So they sped
up an icy slope in a black car. As it jolted to
a stop, the high beams illuminated the
mausoleum. She wanted to change out of
her uniform into a skin-tight, hip-hugging top.
To be something sexy, not Catholic good.
Unbuttoning the winter coat, it was the
first time undressing in front of a boy. She
shivered in the white cotton undershirt, white as
their icy exhales. She put on sexy, but couldn't be it.
Glancing out the window, she saw the shadow of a
man with a black dog going past. She screamed.
They sped down the hill to a sleazy gas station.
She never wanted to see ghosts again, but
he doubted her sanity. 'You're depressed,' he said.
She turned and saw her reflection in the car window.
A face angular and pale, that of a ghost, staring back.

Steven J. Rogers

Blood on the Highway

Figure if leaving is in the future, going to need to clean this pair of pants. Maybe get out the windex and wash the memories from the asphalt.
Scrape up all that blood.
The wind is something to fear. The kind that blows through dirty brown hair, but only when it feels like it. And it don't ever feel like it anymore.
Cold something fierce. Dispatched colors locked inside darkness shortly after they received their marching orders. Unable to escape, despite the exaggerated freedoms of the American highway system.
Drag that rotten turtle corpse out of the ditch. Build it an alter on the margins of black tar sands and flaccid waves. The elderberry branches its pyre. The fire its vessel.
Transcend terrestrial borders through ash.
Used to be this ceremony meant something. Now it's frigid and shallow. There used to be something out here.
It's all condemned. Boarded up and barb wired.
A sign on a post made out of driftwood. A broken canoe filled with potted range flowers. A snake that don't know its tail from its head. Guts shattered and spread like lawn ornaments in a river town.
Seems so long ago these casualties first littered this place.
Root knuckles think they're going to win this war. But none of them are battling anymore.
They scream anyway. They don't know they're too far gone and the memories aren't going away. Their voices sound digital. Infected like

the rest of us.

"Don't come this way. Don't come any way. Ain't no clean pants going to change any of that."

Leverett Butts

Vignettes from Emily's Stitches

One

If you walked through the woods, keeping the creek on your left and went straight 'til you saw the lightning tree what's half dead and bore right, following the foot trail a piece, you'd see my place. Now I didn't live there or nothing, but it was mine just the same. It's where I'd go when I wanted to think about things or just be alone for a while. What it was was an old slave shack from back in the Civil War days, but hadn't nobody lived there in years. Oh, I suppose the occasional hobo'd stop there for a night or two, but I'd never seen one. My daddy told me to stay away from it on account of its being so old and run down. I reckoned he thought it was liable to fall right on my head if I so much as looked at it cross-eyed. But I figured it was safe enough, so I tended to disregard Daddy's wariness and fears and such. Hell, by the time he found out about the place, I'd staked my claim on it about three months.

Two

I had pretty much given up on being able to get lucky with my own personal charms and was just about to swallow my pride and raise three bucks, when she showed up. Literally on my doorstep. When I walked into the shack one afternoon, I found her asleep on the floor of my front room. Of course, I didn't realize she was a girl at the time. I figured her for one of the occasional hobos I never saw spending nights in my place. She was all covered up with tattered blankets, scraps of paper, and old clothes. In fact, I couldn't figure out if she was a hobo or the nest of some hellacious rat king like in that Christmas movie with the Russian ballerina fella.

Three

"My name is Emily, and if you so much as breathe at my father, I swear to God and Moses I'll kill you." Emily Blanchard was fourteen, though you couldn't tell by either sight or sound. Old Jim Blanchard had about a hundred kids, and I didn't think there was any danger of his ever being sober enough to notice her gone until she was at least thirty.

Four

"You mean to tell me you've had a girl stashed up in that old shack for a month now and you ain't tried to do nothing with her?" Gardener hadn't been out to my place for a while. His folks gave him a raise on his weekly allowance, and he'd had better places to spend it. He only showed up this Saturday because Bertha had taken a few days off to go visit her mother and help pay for the old lady's electrolysis. When he saw Emily there, he was surprised, but figured I'd kept the secret to myself in order to get in some good experience without having to share. You should've seen his jaw drop when I told him I hadn't even tried nothing with her. I bet a whole herd of sheep could've fit right between his teeth.
"What in God's good grace is wrong with you boy?" He stammered. "You afflicted or what?"
"No. I just hadn't thought much about it, that's all. I mean she's only fourteen."

"I don't rightly see your point. She's a Blanchard; I'm sure she knows all about it. Besides, even if she were a Rockerfeller, I think an exception could be made for a fourteen year old looking that good."

"Gardener," I said feeling a funny sinking feeling in my stomach. "Ain't you got any morals or common decency at all?"

"Sure I go to church." That wasn't what I had asked him, so I just turned around and went home.

Five

I thought a good deal about what Gardener said the rest of that day. Especially about the fact that she was a Blanchard and probably knew all about it. I thought about Emily not ever telling me why she ran away, and I thought about poor old drunk Jim Blanchard and how he'd been widowed damn near fourteen years. I thought about morality, and how Gardener apparently figured going to church was morality enough. I wondered if it was, but I didn't think so. Besides, Gardener only went to church to try and see up Sister Joyce's skirts when she sat up so high playing the organ. I didn't think that really counted for going to church anyway. That night I had a dream. At first it was like any dream I might have had whenever I felt particularly frustrated. Only this time instead of Anne Marie or even Ol' Lady Simms, It was Emily Blanchard. As soon as I realized it, I got that same funny sinking feeling in my stomach, and I knew it wasn't no ordinary sex dream. Emily really was incredible looking and that made my sinking speed up. I was falling from a great height and I couldn't stop. I couldn't stop. When I did stop, I looked in a mirror that was suddenly right at my head, and I saw Emily under me but she was tied up and she had a bruise on her eye. But that wasn't the most disturbing part of the dream. When I looked at myself in the mirror, I looked like old Jim Blanchard. I made myself wake up.

Six

I went to my place that afternoon. As I neared the place, I realised that everything was real quiet. It was eerie. Then I heard some shuffling coming from one of the shot-out windows, and when I looked, I saw that Gardener was there. All hundred and sixty pounds of him. Emily was there, too. It was just like my dream, only this time I was the mirror. And this time the sinking feeling was rising. I stood transfixed outside that window, my mind a sheet of white. Gardener looked up at me and grinned. I was stuck floating in my stomach rising towards the white in my head. I couldn't do anything until Emily looked, too. She wasn't crying; she wasn't whimpering; she was just there. To this day, I'm not sure how I got through that window so fast. I only know that it took me about three seconds to reach Gardener. He was still grinning like an idiot when I kicked him in the ribs and knocked him over. He was still grinning like an idiot when I straddled his chest and punched him twice in the nose. He was still grinning like an idiot when he flipped me over and grabbed my neck. Neither one of us saw Emily with the two-by-four. She hit him once to knock him off me, and then he took off out the window.

Steven J. Rogers

Bed

Don't forget to drag that thing out to the curb. It's covered in mildew, mold, and there's a little rot. Right along the edge by the small rip with the blood stain.
When it was purchased, the saleslady said to jump on it a little bit. So the form fitting foam that covered the plush top would easily conform to the contours of the body.
There was a joke. Something about fucking. She didn't get it.
Then, there was her — Long tangled hair, offset by Italian anger.
And her — With her stories about life inside of a strip mall.
And her — With her constant jokes and cackling laughter.
And her — The only her.
She took her first fall from there. Got stuck between the broken TV stand and the wall. Flailed there for hours before...
There were more falls. Until she couldn't move anymore. Her remaining legs twisted and use- less. A cosmic joke of failed muscles and time.
Then, she was gone. Then...
Drag that bed to the mountains of rubble. To the detritus of humanity. To the lands filled with broken memories.

Mike Luz

The Sorrow

Novice on windshield
explaining mulch
river sliced
graceful mantras,
byways
hummingbirds
mad flight
into poetry
sizable intrigues
obeying rules
jar's end
a cookie

Wretch

A body is
planted or it
burns, a semicircle
twelve-times triangular
interpreted
prosthetic
aimed at
slogan: shoelace
in search of
spacetime
curves bent back-
ward
out of whack
dirempted
melancholic term papers
claims unanswered
a silent ring
flowers an eyeball
sits on

Edward Manzi

White Marble

I am the white marble in the brown dirt below the flowering tomato plant reflecting the morning sun and the blue sky, smooth and hard in the shadow of something taller, expanding my influence despite staying the same size, looking over my shoulder and imagining I had legs that could get me somewhere, so I wouldn't have to be rolled around by some finger.

Wooden Spoon

Grandma is stirring three gallons of red sauce, as a gasoline-dipped chocolate bunny is burning, sacrificed in front of a skull faced Mary on the old well in the backyard, while the May flies are playing hop-scotch on the dirt road, hoping it will bring them back to the river, never thinking of the trout that will eat them.

From The Abandoned Castle

VI

I am not interested in much that will get me anywhere in the preordained real world of elves. I am still trying to figure out how to get the stripped screw out, that remains firmly in its place.

In the shrubs, two discarded half eaten popsicles are melting. What if my dead body was found in a river under suspicious circumstances? Would it add to my unpredictable legend?

Timothy Hudenburg

without

go on get outside
cooped up as we are
imagining the desolation of March
everything gone silent
gray even the air
cloaks itself into mist
snowdrifts have finally melted
the worn shovel packed
the giant maple out front
gone silent in the season
barren without leaves
even light weakens
what to do with it
look closer into that light
read the meager script
being written
it is so
—

there at the branches
everywhere buds

Christopher Hopkins

Mera Field

And on the stoke,
the honour bell.
A sounding peal across the stow.
The feel of vinyl cafe tops,
the kicks and knocks of pub door swings,
the faithful ping to sound the land
all that line the blunt peach stones.

A ringing in the ear of the war dead,
above the pound shop till ring din.
Our boys and whys almost lost,
like the wrought iron leaf
under council's paint,
on that resting place of brass and reed.

Trace your fingers across their names,
lifted, weathered rubbed,
on the black brass plates upon the gate.
Names still called in classroom shouts,
amongst the team sheet nods,
but lost in a liberty of sorts.

And while dark the soul of the country's heart,
how would the sounding ghosts see their land?
As their reason for endurance or their murder ground?

Such the surrender in this no man's land.
This losing war on red earth floors.

Of hope and strength now unthinkable loads.
Of youth once blind on destiny,
now blinded with allegories,
on the food bank opportunities,
the poor callow fools of the self.
And the old like unwanted books,
bent double from the winding punch of the unseen wounds.

Hearts slitted up like the lungs of old.
The life is death and death holds all,
all in this hideous familiar.
And the pointed bell strikes
with such savage discipline,
sounding past the flag poles and roundabouts,

cafes and the hairdressers,
the white goods and red faces,
the betting shops and the charity whores,
who stand behind their glass counters,
and past the church paths and graveyards still,
tended by nature's hand

and council strimmers.
And like the shot that kills the poet,
the last ring of the hammered chive,
and air comes white with peace.
The senselessness comes to fall,

from lace doilie houses to rotting town hall.

There will be no prayers.
No torch held high.
No chives or bells for now fallen souls.
None shall be remembered.
Just a town pronounced dead,
for the best it is said.

Ricky Garni

Purple Car

The Whole Time I Had a Friend Named Franz
Franz Liszt Never Crossed My Mind

I wish I had a purple car
because it would look so good
as I drove by holding a lemon sherbet cup
People would say: "That's a delightful combination!"
while others might throw their undergarments in joy
Just like they did in the days of Franz Liszt (ca 1800
something.) But not at everybody. Only at Franz.
That sexy man simply knew how to play the piano
like a little God. If you don't believe me, look it up.
Garments were thrown. Ladies fainted.
Blows were exchanged. Blow jobs were exchanged.
A glove was lost. A glove of Franz. Un Petit Dieu!
If I am wrong, you can punch me in the face.
If I am right, you can punch me in the face anyway.
Sometimes I feel like my face could
use a good punch. After all, what have I done
in this life, other than imagine purple and lemon
together, tell you my little stories, with as you were
and I as I was and why – nothing else
If only I could play the piano
like Franz Liszt before he died
and lost one glove

and then another

Someone Stole Anna Pavolova's Slippers

Her ballet slippers and what do you suppose someone is doing with them unless they have feet the size of Anna Pavlova feet that can't dance in them and if they loved them enough to steal them and even if they fit nice and snug they probably aren't dancing with them anyway they love them too much

Anna Pavlova's ballet slippers are in a dusty old shoe box somewhere saying Behold! I am Anna Pavlova's ballet slippers! which you can't hear because of shoebox-tinny voices but they keep saying it anyway they hope something will come of it and they will dance again –

Unlikely, and meanwhile, her regular slippers are under the bed, and the TV is on. At first it's
a commercial for cheese snacks, and then a ride in the country in a Chevy, and then it's some evangelist telling us we must pray to God or you just can't imagine the awful, the awful – you just can't imagine.

Patricia Thornton

Who is Sylvia? What is She?

Today I rang my father
Told him my mother had died
And tears welled in his eyes.

As a child I used to search for him
In the bus station,
Amongst the faces on the underground train
Just in case he was passing
Or lost or had forgotten
His way home.

Today I rang my father
Told him my mother had died
And he audibly wept.

He used to call her Sylvia
Though she was Betty at home
The nurses too said 'Sylvia
We are just turning you
To make you more comfortable.
Is that better Sylvia?'

Today I rang my father
Told him my mother has died
And he sobbed.

One day he wrote a letter,
Told us where he was.
That he lived in Lisbon.
His name is Alan now
Not Bob.

Today I rang my father
Told him Sylvia is dead
And his voice broke on the line.

After the Shakespeare poem she used to play on the piano

Now the Hedges Have Gone

Beyond our reach
First a hunched ball
Strangely still on the open path.

They can't have noticed the open gape
The teeth exposed, the small black leather hands
Close fingered in repose

When the fencing was delivered
and dumped on top
He was hidden from our view.

Later the final piece erected we
Strained to see through the gaps
Evidence of our little hog in vain hope that he still…

And yes there he was prickles, mottled but quite distinct
Bristling against the indignity of it all,
But flat.

Peter Dietrich

The Breaking

Here lie the remnants of the dreams they were given,
Reflected in the dark depths of the ocean,
They wanted to believe their souls would be driven
By some deep force of perpetual motion,
Yet Time was the victor as the mystery was revealed,
And the cast-off spoils were left out for the taking,
The harshness of the light left nothing to be concealed,
While their voices were ignored throughout the breaking.

Soft were the voices which proclaimed the new coming,
With each stranger a possible Messiah,
But the Masters weren't satisfied with the misguided humming,
All wanting their own stars to rise higher,
The readers read the readings that spread yet more confusion,
Sweeping clean past all the noise they were making,
So the spent agony became just one more illusion,
As the first truth was ground down to dust in the breaking.

Jealous were the landscapes they passed through alone,
Wanting to keep more than mere shadows,
But the paths through the forest were vastly overgrown,
With dark corners where no soothing wind blows,
The sun was so low as to burn the smallest bird's wings,
And the deepest roots of the trees were aching,
The procession of non-believers brought their own offerings,

While the empty footprints were simply devoured by the breaking.
Fierce were the warriors who proclaimed the world set free,
As the spinners-of-tales were all defeated,
But the eyes in the darkness just couldn't let it be,
When the sorry lamentations were repeated,
The sword and the word then became battling brothers
In a fight even the innocent were forsaking,
The children were corrupted by the surrogate mothers,
Their flowing tears completely ignored by the breaking.

Timid was the night of the last ongoing struggle,
When all the players ignored the main goals,
They tried to regroup in the abandoned cathedral,
As though the rituals might still save their souls,
The book and the candle remained on opposite sides,
While the sermons were so obviously faking,
The mercenaries broke in where the sacred light resides,
And the real obscurity became truth through the breaking.

Here shines the promise of the dream they resurrected,
Blazing like a temple in the sun,
They chose to believe in the master they'd elected,
Knowing all the other webs had been spun,
The false words were banished to the halls of outwitted shame,
While the lovers came together in the awaking,
Tyranny lost all its powers so could no longer blame
Those who knew better than to kneel before the breaking.

Ajibola Tolase

Dust

Revisiting places where we once shared a secret
brings my father air in the picture of him I carry.
At the lake, he would insist we wait until everyone leaves
else the moment won't be exact.
We would walk further till my father is convinced
we are back there in time and it was happening again:
the kiss locked in memory,
she is there, my mother, twirling around him.
He said here is where water holds us on its plane, your mother and I.
Before a painting of the war at the museum
he said everything is so real now. He pointed at the ruin of a city
he said the church he married in was there and
a fountain of losses at another spot.
He said everything is dust now you know, me too.

Discovering psalms

So the songbird sings of the city below the sea.
Perhaps it's on the same water that I learnt

what it means to travel with home in my pocket.
Ours is a house of songs. Father,

a bald musicologist fingered his piano for a ballad
before an open window

through which we bore witness to the aesthetic
array of cloud layers.

Other days, you could catch father asleep
with a rhythm clutched to his chest.

Mother, a songsmith, usually bent over a wet floor
or broken china thinks of kintsugi as an art of renewal.

But that was early, before the voyage through the sea
in search of a hymn.

Father could have sworn he heard the sea say his name
at the coda of his performance,

of course I should write from inception:
Father steered our boat clear off known places,

to cut through morning haze into a museum of songs.

Arrayed as artefacts in their cases, 150 of them, awaiting an audience.

Father, lost in an epiphany, arched his head at an angle
as if to align his ears with the frequency of water.

He entrusted the oars to me in a sea where I am no captain,
we plunged deeper into the water:

here's a school for learning the enigma in the creation of Pisces,
designed as though there's a foretelling

of water as a home of songs such that squiggle too is a dance move
—this we know as ritual.

The inequality of grace puts father in a class of saints.
I return, with a plethora of dirge, to mother who is now broken.

Natalie Crick

Rose

Today I drift through an apple orchard,
Calloused and scabbed,

Branches bent in silver and gold
While the sun sets on the prairie,

Rousing the dead.
Some nights
It rouses me too.

Sweet low hanging fruit,
Break your skin for me.

Each meagre flower is thin,
Sparse of leaf,

More precious
Than a single Rose,

Lifted in the crisp wind,
Pale as moon-shell.

The deep blue Violets
Flutter on the hill.

Violet,
Your grasp is frail,

But you catch the light;
A star edged with frost and fire.

One hundred years of you
Is just enough, yet not enough to see

Full beauty beyond its frame,
And name this life yours to love.

Norman Miller

Ape-Leader

Ape-leader - n. an old maid: their punishment after death, for neglecting increase and multiply, will be, it is said, leading apes in hell
                    1811 Dictionary of the Vulgar Tongue

I

Men are neanderthals, God's toys
set one step in on evolution's coil.
I am the carnage at their centre,
a dark galactic core, wheeled around,
ticked off with a Universal hiss.

The apes come, fallout on a breeze.
They say love is a balm, enough to calm
Lazarus scuttling from his opened cage.

My sisters are fostered, cultured, sculpted into shape,
Nothing new. I watch the tea-party squabbling,
noise, breakage, staying silent until the blood stops.

II

The apes are older now: I've led them long, my troupe,
a poor cast strung out, cans on a bumper,
clattering applause on grey bitumen.

No escape: they tag along,
a chain-gang on the road to now.
One day we make the tracks, then
kiss the boulders we once broke.

It is all stupid, this progress through love.
No sense, yet it fills all senses.
When it cracks, some snatch
for male holders:
reduced to dirt, I'm borne
on men's hard shoulders.

Anthropological Notes on the Lost Tribes Date: 2067

Note 1 (location not recorded)

The Wattiz scarred their skin near death
a shield of magic leaving their body a pure husk
in the knowledge of the tribe

The Wattiz scarred their skin near death
allowing evil parts to be cast
shrivelling in the dry air of the desert
where they increasingly lived

Their shamen were selected
at birth unchallenged to lay down
what may or may not be said.
Power was used to subdue desire

Their poetry, their lore
was seeing through squinting eyes.
It is not known what part does the telling tale
and what part does philosophise.

Note 2 (location - coastal Old England)

The Norong stood tall like ostrich
waving & running, running

they roared for the burning
of witches, who they daub

& blame for the dark smoke & the stinking
flesh that blinds them
whenever fires were lit.

Note 3 (location uncertain – possibly Middle East)

The Notwe and the Norong share
a poetry to say always an other thing,
to spy the alien from without
the campfire's circle:

where is the edge of me?
learned by osmosis
the groaning of bones

Note 4 (location North America – Eastern Seaboard)

The Notwe and the Norong did strut the same ranges,
herding the same animals.
Each felt threatened as they threatened.

In the Notwe laughter was insult.
In the Norong there was none.

They wear amorphous faces in their war dance
shifting expressions of form and plumage.
To speak & to weep are barely distinguished.

War Child

'Rape is often used in ethnic conflicts as a way for attackers to perpetuate their social control and redraw ethnic boundaries.'
                                        Amnesty International

The sky is big and blue like me.
My blood's stopped coming,
messaging from my inner space
before you were on top, your gun
at ease by a fetid bed.

I stare up into heaven's gut
find no ease, no defended place.
Retreating, I scroll defilements.

You touched the rib beneath my breasts
in this anti-Eden, and sowed me with hard static:
stench, sperm and immolation.
Everything teaches something, even storm-hearts,
plumes of far horses riding.

We hang by a thread,
my stomach a curved drum you beat.
You are my broken fragment,

matter snaking in on a tightrope,
coiling, uncoiling.

Your water – mine - is clean.
Come quick when I lie spread, forsaken.
Distract me, love: bring this in your coming.
And cry when you are hit -
it is the start of learning.

Tom Stevens

Situation in the Early Stages in the Air and on the Coast

They have the cities of the coast.
Eyes, struck out and dulled, laugh in tandem
With gaping, enormous jaws.
We've seen them train boys to fight
And put them to war
In the crest of the clouds,
Skimming thunderheads with steel
Before trailing down, down.
They come streaking across the sea with sails made of skin,
An all too believable serpent striking the bay.
We have to shelter in swamps and mud pits
While the sky is broken, piece   by   piece
You can't look at the sky too long,
The bay burns. The sand is glass now,
Villages are rounded up, elders baked
In mounds of dung, babes hooked up
And electrocuted. Bikes are filled with filthy diesel
To smoulder into the heartlands.

They have the cities of the coast,
Dull struck-out eyes and gaping jaws laughing-
They have the cobble streets
Where I have pushed barrows and hauled soil
And sprawled with the olders, the youngers,
Before the dry, worn & scarred hides made it onto the horizon

Of sea and sky and land
                    –and took branches from the tree.

I wonder – do they step into the after-life,
Necronautical, aboard dulled and soot-stained ships
That scream into the silence- do they march out there
To follow the infantry and sailors and citizens
That they have falsely lain to rest?

They are shooting at the trucks! Crossing the riverlands, drenched in red crosses,
Green writing reading 'medical.' No one can be saved if the medics are fired upon.
We are neutral; we go to aid the invaders, but how do you save someone cackles at their own amputation, or vomits while smiling, or collects the scalps of the dead and the ears of new slaves? They shoot at the convoy, and, one by one, the trucks veer uncontrollably to the side of the road.

Han't seen the sun shine for a while.
Years? Months? I can't tally that tackles,
Got nowt to mark, cept my owns flesh.
One village is grey rubble and silence,
Dusty. Not even corpses left to attracts
Dogs to get in mud and flies and noise
And lay turds in their wake and bring in
Grass an rats and shrubs.
They sow stillness in their bootprints…
In the next village a toothless woman weeps over the
Dark and blotchy corpse of a young babe.

I looked upon my own wee lad once,
Under the sun. Before the sky tore open,

And the ocean blackened,
Before their marching chant
Consumed all and excreted forth void;
Dismiss this life, worship death
Dismiss this life, worship death
Dismiss this life, worship death

David Lohrey

Black and Blue

First the sky, black or blue, depending on the time.
By day, Memphis blazes, 100 degrees in the shade; the sky,
Robin blue.
At night, there are lightning bugs galore and stars, eerie,
Dazzling and quiet, as from the Mississippi, slaves once
Dragged bales across cobblestones.

Color of my eyes? My mother's?
It was morning glories we beheld, not roses. Roses
Come in black, not in blue. I did see father many times
But I don't remember his eyes.

White and black photographs show us in our pajamas
With little bows and arrows scrawled across the tops.
Bugles and drums decorate our blue bottoms.
Snow cones at Tobey Park were that hue, too.

All gone now: how large the Pippin loomed over the police academy.
German shepherds lunged at padded arms as men in black
Set fires with smoke as thick as cotton candy. Heading back,
We devoured ten cent burgers at Fred Montesi's and pocketed
Beatles cards at the Woolworths.

From 2 to 6, TV's Happy Hal hawked fantastic wigs to kids
Like me with giant waxen lips. Friday nights, close to midnight,

Boris Karloff, our best friend, dropped in for chips and dip
And stolen Tootsie Pops.

The Pink Palace was dad's fortress of art and power,
In costumes he designed himself: a clown, some whimsy,
A melancholic smile, despair, or an oriental stare;
In make-up and girdles, a sword, a pistol, a tunic or robe,
Tights and sandals, shaped from plastic or leather.
Father directed: Give them some cleavage. Show 'em your tits.

Dress rehearsal: You'll eat it and like it.
Get your ass over here, or no dinner for you.
Mrs. Rosenthal? She wants the part?
Goddamn it! Would somebody get her the fucking script?
The actors above; a black man below, bathing in the
Basement ditch, a smelly remnant of Jake's endeavors.
Dad still at it: Stop talking and bring me two aspirin.

I read the reviews of the greatest show on earth.
The boosters took stock:
"It is a miracle, stupendous, a brilliant start."
The theatre was packed; no one could get in.
He was selling tickets, ten bucks a shot
To crawl through the attic, to stand at the back.

Not wanting to stay—please no longer. Not one more hour,
Not another minute, not five measly seconds more.
My mother couldn't get out of town fast enough.
She tried to quit drinking, to stop punishing herself,
For allowing him to insist on yes, always to demand the store.

That father could ruin a dinner for a lousy buck is true.

Kool-Aid or pudding? Take one or the other. He saved 50 cents
At Morrison's and lost my love. The grand master had little to give;
It was all show but no tell. I'll have another martini.

Don't disturb his rest, dear mother cried. This is our house.
Get out!
So I reached out my five-year-old hand, and fled from Tennessee.
Why are you calling? How dare you ask for money!

It feels right that the old man is dead. His heart was black and blue.
He beat himself up and beat me, too.
When I think of Memphis I think of death, but not from long ago
And not from yellow fever.
Brother Martin was first to go and then Vernon Presley's loving son.

This December, the trees in our yard will come down,
Felled by an ice storm, torrential and freezing. Birds will be heard,
Not chirping but mocking.
Dad's gone now, thank goodness; there's only mother left.
The dogwoods stand silent, as her eyes watch, laughing.
There's much comfort knowing how much she loves the bluff.

Beside The Red Barn

Beside the red barn
at an intersection
between today and tomorrow,
 a man from Alabama
 plays the banjo
 on his knee;
 he whistles Dixie
 and wears a Confederate cap
 with shoes by Nike.
 Roy Rogers, his uncle,
 stands stark naked
 on his bed
 eating a Milky Way,
 with a red bow on his penis;

 His second wife Maybelline
 won't quit laughing.

Daniel Boone and
Davy Crocket
 embrace with affection.

The mayor of San Antonio cries quietly at attention.
It's Thursday afternoon at 3.

Outer Space

Jason has disappeared from my vision.
Then there's Michael.
Marian is gone, then mom and dad.
One by one they go.
Soon: no one.

I feel like the man on the moon.
The astronaut left to drift, holding
His severed umbilical cord, gasping;
Earth at a distance, disappearing.
I'm going, getting smaller and smaller.

I'm saying hello but no one can hear me.
Like Marilyn Monroe or Cher's husband,
Sonny. Lost in space, the movie. It
Opens in September.
Lost forever, the nightmare: 24/7.

I've arrived at the lost and found,
But I can't remember what I came for.
Sign here.

There were once so many;
I could name them but why bother?
Some leads, but mainly a chorus, a jubilee, not a party.
More like a camp fire without marshmallows.
A cookout, without charcoal; a broken nail with no file.

Tits without ass. A pocket with no money.

How the hell did it happen?
Oh, it's one decision after the other.
Choices.
Ingratiation, followed by despair.
Indoctrination, then disappointment.
It's leaving home in a hurry.
It's a flat tire on the highway.
It's a bridge too far.
Emasculation.
It's not 2+2=4.
It's not oppression, not control.
Not intervention, not suppression,
Not even repression, no.
It's indifference.
The tyranny of neglect.
It's choking on nothing.
It's a phone call to We Care,
Only We Care is moving.
Call back tomorrow.
By the time you get through,
Your problems are over.
Leave your name after the beep.
By the time you get through,
It's been settled.
Press 'O' for operator assistance.
By the time you get through,
You're finished.

How may we direct your call?

Julia Rose Lewis

Transcript of the Hieratic

Behold the reader
chess pieces in his pockets
gift from the arts gods
Oh my god in black ink, how did this pinecone get so big? The word elephant became
equivalent to elegant in the head so mind the pinecone among the candles. In deed, the elegant
sloth. Let me be an epiphyte, let us not repeat fine, if forest green is hunter green with blue here.
Teeth are less interesting than language and trunks. The prehensile lips of horses can at least
separate corn from sweet feed the picky eaters. The oldest cow is known as the matriarch of the
group. Sit and whisper down the lane to sanity: one guinea pig, two guinea pigs, no more guinea
pigs. Pinecones must be cooked to be fed to guinea pigs. Think from a modified leaf.
golden larch and fir
in fibbonacci numbers
bract scales or seed scales

Dear Bear

you held me in sunlight
nervous so shiny as
black patent leather.
Dear phorophyte, you have held me in the light. Fair play, the apple-shaped pear is not to reunite
as sinister. Neither bear nor rottweiler, the skin on a ripe asian pear has the color of a rottweiler's
points.
Let me be epinephrine not a parasite. Play fair against the loss of neurons that secrete
norepinephrine in the sympathetic nervous system. Fearing the shuffling trot, like a horse with
navicular changes, so goes the Parkinsonian gait. You might as well ride a bear or a rottweiler.
So just fault the three year old for calling a rottweiler a bear; the traditional gait of the rottweiler
is the trot. A prototype of oil slick black fur, my prayer to the bear, the peer, and the phorophyte:
let us pause on the lawn before the line of trees.

Hieratic

Some texts embody resonance hybrids by fencing it inside big square brackets:
carbon dioxide. We hate it,
but trees grow in the shape of brackets.
To draw resonance structures of
carbon dioxide: we respire it.
Double headed arrows are used
to draw breath,
a hybrid of two or more fictitious Lewis structures.
Double headed arrows are used,
but trees grow in the shape of nervcus systems;
this hybrid is more stable than its fictitious Lewis structures.
Some texts embody resonance in the heads of Cerberus in big square brackets.

Sarah Kathryn Moore

1 Vanishing Point

their heart grew cold
they let their wings down
                    —Sappho, trans. Anne Carson, Fragment 42

Evening arrives and I am far away, on a mountain covered in flowers, on a knucklebone funneling to plate-eyed Saint Lucia, blonde braids infinitesimally unpinning. Back home, our balcony windows the fulvous tree where patchwork-skirted Lady Margery perches, blowsily whispering, vermillion, vermillion, until it's ochre blooms in my brain, and you, invincible, scalene. Paralysis of touch: you're nettle. Paralysis of great rain, long spell of teeth dreams, weirdly frequent frayed hems. In the year of the lighthouse, what we miss can sink ships. In the year of hive-living, to taste almond in the apple seed means it's never over. Still—what hostage is growing at the empty home in the early evenings, giving us bad dreams, neuroses? Paralysis of fate: I'm false wife. Paralysis of waking up for a drink of water, to stand in the kitchen hostage of the body that can't go into the kitchen because it is already in the kitchen. To stand with doghead Christopher in a wash of blue, to be rinsed in it, field of lavender, bone and bone china, forests-worth fragments of the true cross. Field of human rind: to know oneself fallen, to be fell with it. Field of Catharine wheel I am on and apart from at once, watching someone else—it's you I love—splinters of lemongrass filling my eyes. The saints grow blunt. Their hearts are cold. We love, as far as they can see, but through eyes gemmed with fluke, with truant surf, can we blink away the salt. The saints begin to shave us from their hearts; they preen, comb their wings of us. Night falls in the grim room where every stone is turned and every spool is wound and no wound is owned, we asked for this, earned it, into the brim, the breach. Every day two less minutes light.

2 Validation

We placed the cactus in the gallery and wrapped it in barbed wire to give it extra protection, at the same time giving it our love. We waited to see if it would drop its thorns [...]
—Marina Abramović, on her artwork Luther

Reassurance, we need so much of it!—roving the dream museum, stalking, seldom seeing. The pine box levitates in the center of the empty room, bathed in red light, uvular, limpid: still I'm blue: nnnngggg is the word I think of when I think of you. We call out caveats, we warn, Shark shark shark!, we say, baby, I'm toxic, and not metaphorically. I glimpse you in the black gallery. We are unable to perform. Instead we build two black vases the size of our bodies. One vase reflects the light; the other absorbs it. This is not overly reassuring. We try again, tipping our head and chest against the mineral pillows, beneath whom lounging Saint Carlos Gardel, suavely eyebrowed smiling. Combing corridors thieving magic objects for each other: chairs for lovers, geodes, scissors, materials (copper, iron, wood, pig blood and human hair); also the death self. Leopard-crawling from the death self, we enter the sound corridor. "Jealousy," a tango, is being played repeatedly and loudly. We remain motionless until our outstretched arms eventually sink down. We sink into the desert. The desert reduces you to yourself. That's all that happens. Sitting in front of the amethyst crystals without moving.

Lying in front of the amethyst crystals without moving. Breathless with human transformative capacity. Waiting for a solution. The lethal, blade-rung ladders in a domed stone room floored with sand lead to curved large windows. I am climbing the ladders. You smoke. Duration: limitless.

3 Vivisection

Syr, ye schal welyn sum day that ye had wept as sor as I.
—from the Book of Margery Kempe

Everyone wants to be desirable in her own cohort and this girl was no different: tally of the girl's nights a solid win for clean sheets. But her throat was always open and the sisters whispered, See how she pours out the Name! During her early years it was thus, and she herself a fount of grace, shut drawer, executrix of her own estate. Tuning-forklike she struck herself on the world and the world wowed back, her name the act of pouring oil from a pitcher to a dish. The sisters husked and pundled; but though the girl loved them, a certain chemise charisma kept her edging. She prayed to have the word vehement so deeply driven into her heart she could get no relief until God taught her its meaning. Then one night God showed up in a throng of shucks, a glitter shower, cusses of coppers pouring from the sky. It was very nice! But all she got when God was gone was phantom scent of sour wine and Satsuma, and then the wanting feeling started, so that by the time spring came, her body sweet and heavy the girl was walleyed and deranged with waiting. On the world-map countries were fragments of candy, all jewel-tone and sugar straight the brain. One eye darted and her ankles were painful. The sisters started tching. She wanted to be called some name like David, etched in the ache of it. She wanted to love the French language, how *again* can mean yet can mean still. The sisters have long moved away. But the girl remains, practicing a sort of phrenology—they say I'm a doctor now—(Saints Emma and Anna note what's changed, the heart's shape, bracelets made from cutlery are no longer chic)—can you see her? Standing at the canted edge of your body, eyelash-fine and pure as blood?

Elizabeth Lasch

Slink

Creep—
Creeping.
Momentary fright.

Seep—
Seeping.
The lacquered beast
Dost bite.

All things you fear
Take form in metal.
They still your heart—
So tremors settle.

The leafy eyes of Eden
Have been banned beyond your sight.
In place, you see their reddened pit—
Devoid of silky light.

Hail

Take your languid loutish lies,
Release them within a storm.

Watch them grow and screech and roar.
They're taking your true form.

Let lies prowl, let lies promise,
Let liars bleed, although they're bloodless.

Yet liars hold a saddening charm,
Unbeknownst to me.
Through decrepit, void like, forlorn caverns—
Their lies make light to see.

Sugar

Some people fall in love with beauty.
Where there may be beauty, deception soon follows.
Seemingly, in the end we have succumb to love deception.

Michael Lehman

If the Wild Geese Ever Learned to Read

If the wild geese ever learned to read
they'd be subject to passport control, immigration
sanitary codes, compulsory education, taxes
In a few words their way would be gone from the sky

Geese in apartment buildings
Geese on welfare or limping home from work
Drunk geese, dull broken feathers
Geese shooting each other with pistols
The young birds on the street getting into cars
with creepy foie gras chefs

The geese walked out of dinosaur cities
and one of them was the first to fly
There's no evolution without genius, without
miracles. That's what wings are

For a Witch

She spreads out
like cloud following the creeks

The brambles
aided by a straw broom
grow tangled and more lovely
beneath the quiet flying
of a sleepy evening song

It's no great secret
the hills made the people
so the people would make the hills

The stalk of meadow grass
bending down a crown of seeds
the woman in her bed
with nonsense on her lips

Shoelaces

A single peach suspended in midair above the Swingline stapler plant in Queens, New York

Of all the empty paper bags, one was inside out and ugly

The street is full of people who don't want to sing
Part man, part building, bearing in these bricks a hard aluminum heart
Men chewing gum from off the sidewalk
Men falling asleep in handcuffs
with chips of concrete under their fingernails
These sons of bitches with crumbs hanging out of their mouths
Have you ever eaten your own shoelaces, both of them, slowly, in anger?

Along the Spine

Hit a deer
on route fifteen
I cussed and hit the blinkers
She was down in the road
just a fawn
watching me walk up
a huge dark eye
long black lashes
silhouetted in twilight
Mom on the high bank
watching too no doubt
"I'm sorry," I said
Knelt down and put my hand
on the back of her neck
warm fur
soft as milk

Along the spine
tension and strength
fascia and sinew
life in the mountains
"You've got to get out of the road," I said
'Even if it's just to die,' I thought
Took hold of the skin on her back
and heaved her on her feet
she took a few steps backwards
and fell down

I clapped my hands
and she jumped up
and went bounding after mom
The road was empty as I drove away
raised my hand to my face
there was no odor

To His Dog

I touch your paw
and see a dream about the river
heartbeat green of alder leaves
shadows on the gravel shifting

There was a city that hadn't been built
or a party that had gone on too long
a city failing
we went upstream of that

Swam deep under moss
Smooth redwood and stone
asleep in the whirlpool of deep time
assume shapes lucid as live fish

You and me are all the water
we brought from California

What They Left

Lilac brush
curled tin
graves

The pit
tailings in a white fan
streams all in confusion

A woman by the road
selling pine needle baskets

Rani Drew

Eye to Eye

The small turtle is rehabilitated in a plastic box,
a miniature grassland, carefully
insulated from the surroundings.
Encircled by water, a biggish granite stone
like a highland sits in the centre.

When the timed lamp switches on, like
the Sun rising in the eastern sky,
the miniature turtle moves its forelegs,
one before the other, climbing the height
slowly and steadily to sunbathe in the full light.

I watch it making its way up the stone,
stretching each limb in turn, forward and upward,
until it reaches the rough top, and
hugging the high point, as if atop a mountain,
it sprawls full length for a soak in the sun.

Suddenly it becomes aware of two eyes,
raises its head and looks at me, a lone figure
in the falling darkness of the room. Our eyes meet,
still and searching, without word or motion.

In the silent heat of the lamp, we sit divided
by the box, free and imprisoned,

our thoughts on the riddle of existence.
The room darkens, the lamp switches off.

Sergio Ortiz

Postcards

Yo fui la más callada
de todas las que hicieron el viaje hasta tu Puerto.
Julia de Burgos, Yo Fui la Mas Callada

Willie, when Eloy showed me the wedding rings
I broke out in tears. I was so innocent, didn't even know
why I followed you to Bolivia.

2.

Write me a poem that will bring me back to life, papi.
Be my distraction, or I am going to find a tall, blue eyed angel
with baker hands and lips like James Dean.

A dormir se van ahora mis lagrimas
por donde tu cruzaste mi verso.

3.

Negro, I've murdered myself so many times the effort is starting to hurt.
Someone stole my poetry. They wanted to teach me to write on paper.
As if everything I do isn't already written in blood.
I begged mama to help me die, but she refused,
had to slash my own wrist.

*Todos los ojos del viento
ya me lloraron por muerta.*

4.

Do you think ghosts can ask for asylum in Cuba?
Willie, take my clothes off. Look at my scars
without crying and tell me I'm beautiful. Don't lie,
don't cry. I need to drink a cup of coffee with you
reading me Ginsberg, Simic, and Julia de Burgos.

Yours forever, The Ghost.

---

*the verses in italics are lines from Julia de Burgos's poems

The Martyrdom

One hundred and thirty-six mirrors
whirled around him
like a hurricane, the reflection
of his heart on The Hand
that shapes existence.

Mountains gathered around a line
of blood. Radioactive chain reaction
dripped from his open wounds, and I
despaired. He left me dressed
in shades of purple, aflame,
lowered back into my coffin.

The Smell of Sulfur

The odor of sulfur
is as strong as the company
brought to the podium of Titans.
Gaia and Ouranos spit
angry epithets at each other
in the armory on Boulevard
where the effigy hides
bottles of gin.

On television, the rib-tickling,
righteous Titan gets an opportunity
to explain the notion of drowning
in the desert to the nation
recently targeted by white supremacist.

The program furthers
The Graven image's intent
to build a wall. Is it to keep some out,
or trap everyone in?

Women tip-toeing north
through the desert
leave an uncomfortable trail of blood
too long to ignore,
rivers of pearls buried under the roots
of ancient saguaros on Cristero soil.

Words pronounced
by the Shebang Smoking Idol
don't mean a thing
to thirty million butterflies.
They were there first.

Rose Knapp

Compounded Pronoia

I don't believe in any of you
But fortunately that die is all
Red and cast was slaughtered
Seven Seasons ago but sure
Let's have another just do it
Inspiration is insidiously key
Isn't it? Interest. Who said that?
Meltdowns are what capital is
Made of Kierke/four

Ἄλφα βῆτα Ὠμέγα

La Cosa Nostra Dumas
Life ist performative Plato
Smoke spews from pews
Xcept when das ist nacht
Aristotle ArabiAlles Gha
Zalli Zoroastrian Vespucci
Flesh flies from bones
Sands devour sky
Scrapes futures &
Smurphys get used
To it all Alpha Beta
Omega Kapital
Machismos
Machinas
'Merica
Metric

ADavidic CEShrine

After
Davidic
Draconic
Ank Kah
Sizes
Seas
SenSei
Azures
And
Laughs
At ape
Machina
Attempts
At Crete
Liches
Leeches
Lithium
Lilith
Laconic
Leftbros
Lesbos
Textures
Textstores
Fade to
Crimson
Grim Grime
Gimmlet
Shots & Store

Windows
Wind two
Dao Apples
Deconstruct
Te-Ching
Their cores
Into dark hole
Dust & dark
Matter
WMatthews

Query: [Insert]

Convention
[Conversation]
Why is it cathedrals
It is almost always
Classically train
Of thoughts
Of thought sim
I'm Curious curators plz
Do not give me feedback
I have zero tolerance four
With or for your meatbags
But I am still curious why
Americans & Euros & Japs
Are why is it we all ways go
Back When
They
Have
All
Read
The
Same
Fucking
Terms
&Comm
And
Ments
...

Et Filiii Nostra

In a way it feels so socially
Conditioned to feel wrong
I have not been here in aegis
Pavlov domes paved over with
Pristine prisms of marble icons
Petras encircling parishioners
Does it not Marian Sanctus
Pauline Glorias of past ages
Devout Jerome Spiritus Nihilio
In no nomine Patris Marcion
Etc Filii et Spiritus Sancti
Frozen sunlit rays dust atoms
Hanging in space like the faces
Sybil and Eve supposedly kill
Etc Vulgate dealing psychedelics
Coke and opium inside dens of
A Neo-Baroque candle lit elect
Hushed reverberating service
Echoes of echolalia throughout
Cathedrals unfit for Cathars or
Pagan praxis flux despises doxa
It is not poetry's place to ask
If there's pleasure in the
Fifth commandment
Being unwritten and
Amended instantly
Constantinople but

From one lover to an
Other blank Yeats the
Sensation is as excruciatingly
Sweet as crushing a black berry
And watching the blood static filter
Down through the algorithms and
Onto the coke starved logical
Tongues

Cornelius Rosewater

Tuesday?

I was hurrying out of the bookstore
with my backpack
when the alarm sounded

there were two women in front of me
an older old woman and a younger old woman

the younger old woman heard the alarm
stopped walking and said
what is that beeping? is that us?

stepping quickly past them, I said
no, I believe that that was me

the older old woman
took one look at me and said
well, you certainly look guilty

I laughed and said
yeah, I get that a lot
it must be the hair

and all three of us laughed
before walking off
to wherever life would have us next

as I made my way around

the back of the building, I thought
well, one of us must be guilty

I don't mind
if it's me

today

Everyone, Everywhere

They are
talking
snapping
itching
scratching
hard

they go
latching
onto anything
that helps them
to forget

not one
of them
is really happy
being
alive
being
anything
anywhere
anymore

they all
roam
sob
shamble

spend and
spend

and
spend

and
complain

these
poor fools

these
Rosewater – 5
starving ghosts
thinking
praying
believing
they could
actually
buy life
back

and death,
it comes

with them
never
recognizing

never

realizing or
understanding
the sheer
simplicity
of it all

they die
they go

never
knowing
how

they forged
their chains

they bound
their wrists

they cut
their throats
themselves

Joe Grantham

Barefoot Blues

I rarely go barefoot anymore.
Around the house, the backyard, maybe.
My wife complains when I do.
Never when guests are over, or at the local pool.
Looks can kill.

I live far away from skyscrapers, office buildings, cathedrals,
and miles from orchards and farms.
You could walk barefoot on the streets of my neighborhood,
They are that clean, but I don't.

Leaf blowers, wielded in the hands of landscape artists, rage
Against the machine of boredom and the religion of domesticity.
Bazooka blowers with their gasoline backpacks
Groom the façade of our so-called perfect lives.

On patios surrounded by granite outdoor kitchens with canopies,
Neighbors barbeque on propane grills.
"Because it's cleaner," they yelp.
"I'll take wood, fire, and smoke," I say.
The argument begins.
While I drink beer
Parents brag about their children in med school, law school, tech start-ups, MFAs.
Over glasses of Merlot they steal winks at those

They'll slink off with later only to
Cry on the same shoulders about one who left for good.

I cannot sit barefoot with these people.
Come morning you'll find them in yoga tights slurping Frappacrappos
Infused with caramel and crushed ice
Topped with a glacier of whipped cream.

In my backyard beneath the weeds and two dead birch trees,
Gophers built an underground empire.
I marched across the top of it looking for entry holes the other day.
Felt like walking on a Memory Foam mattress.
With the grass burnt and gone, I took a pick axe to the yard
In an attempt to destroy their kingdom.
I found nothing.
Maybe they moved on to conquer another yard.
Such is my life.

I mow my front yard barefoot just to say, "Fuck it."
To take a chance, to risk, to live dangerously, to feel something.
My wife hates it when I do this.
She says I can drive myself to emergency room next time.
She means it too, but she doesn't appreciate the feel of grass
On bare feet like I do.

Amanda emerges from behind her Volvo across the street.
She's taking her Labradoodle, Goldendoodle, Fuckadoodle,
I can't remember which and don't care, for a walk.
She starts to wave, stops, makes a face
Like I've insulted her dog by calling it a Cockadoodle.

Then I notice her eyes down on my bare feet.
As I stand proudly behind my Toro mulching mower,
Return my best "Have a nice day" smile, and wave.
I yank the cord, the Toro hums to life like a single prop plane.
I push and buzz across the zoysia, over remnants of my scattered
DNA: blood, nails, skin, flecks of bone,
Wondering if I'll lose another part of myself today.

Cornelius Rosewater

The Bug

I am always skeptical
when someone tells me,
you have to meet so and so
I just know
that you will like them

so when this last one
turned out as I expected
it wasn't much of a surprise

for starters
he was already gone
by the time I arrived

by which I mean he was there
and not there
roaring drunk but
not in a good way

he came up to me
like we'd met before
and said through too big a smile
so the bug bit you, too

and thinking he was talking about

chlamydia
which was going around

something awful then
I said
no, man
I'm clean

and he said
no, man
the travel bug
I heard you've been runnin'
all over the world

and I laughed and said
oh, yeah
Rosewater – 7
I suppose so

he smiled and said
yeah man
that travel bug…

there wasn't much to say
after that

it's just funny
how most people are a punchline
to a joke they'll never know

when I left I was still
laughing
at it
at him

at the idea

travel bug
that's cute

here I had always felt
it was more
of a fool's quest

some deadly,
errant crusade

much less of a bug
much more a plague

Natalie Crick

Rose

Today I drift through an apple orchard,
Calloused and scabbed,

Branches bent in silver and gold
While the sun sets on the prairie,

Rousing the dead.
Some nights
It rouses me too.

Sweet low hanging fruit,
Break your skin for me.

Each meagre flower is thin,
Sparse of leaf,

More precious
Than a single Rose,

Lifted in the crisp wind,
Pale as moon-shell.

The deep blue Violets
Flutter on the hill.

Violet,
Your grasp is frail,

But you catch the light;
A star edged with frost and fire.

One hundred years of you
Is just enough, yet not enough to see

Full beauty beyond its frame,
And name this life yours to love.

Claire Scott

Until I Couldn't

I sang to you my son
you loved Burl Ives
way up yonder above the moon

you smiled & sailed past Aquarius
in your batman suit, pointed ears,
blue cape I loosened as you slept

now no lullabies can ease your nights
no songs can untangle your body
torqued & twisted

no way up yonder to transport you to
a place without crutches and opiates
a place without a texting driver

a sudden thud, your body sailing
through space, smacking the street
as sirens slash the night

I want to sing back time
to the child you once were
asleep in your batman suit

but only a moonless night

---

an empty voice
a blue cape lost long ago

My father: The Little Man

we can't see his teeth
his lips curled tight
we can't see
his white polished teeth
he was so proud of
flossing and brushing
with Pepsodent
twice each day
his breath minty
when he kissed us
which was rare
mostly he ignored us
too noisy, too messy
but on our birthdays
we got a special gift
from "the little man"
a stick figure drawing
signed the cards
as though he couldn't
love us directly
as though he needed
a him-not-him
to give us birthday gifts
we pretended not to know
it was he, all the while
knowing he knew we knew
knowing we knew he knew

one year a mickey mouse watch
with glow-in-the-dark hands
another a scarab bracelet
with sacred stones of renewal
birthday photos show
his wide smile
his white teeth
which are now
nowhere in sight
no glow in this dark
no stones of rebirth
for the him-not-him
lying in the bed

Unbearable

I can't bear to see his black-bruised eye
the jagged slash on his cheek still oozing

blood, I can't bear to see his tender smile as
if it never happened: no fight, nothing

thrown, no ER, no lies to the young doctor
about tripping and cutting himself

no knowing I was bourbon-blitzed &
hurled an empty bottle that caught

his face, me with usually lousy aim
for once made a perfect throw

I can't bear to see him checking mirrors,
elevator doors or the flat side of a knife

looking away when he sees me watching
so I won't feel like the-wretched-excuse-of-a-wife that I really am

I no longer let him touch me
I sleep sleepless on the shabby

sofa, in the tight hours
of after-that-night

I can never forgive him for
what I did to him

C. R. Resetarits

Like Haast's Last

Now know this sort of love as hints and tricks,
as feathers, talons, as flutter sounds in
old poems to warn of coming blows.
Finally, we took to wing, took not to
struggle too much against our own rare,
brilliant gravity, whistling through space
like fallen stars, bits of broken worlds as we
re-entered common air and then expired.

All right.
Close eyes. Spin round. Feel the darkness,
movement, comfort of our high-sided nest
one last time. Listen, fancy how pledges fly.
What we conjured was easy spent and lost
next breath, next field, which we will once more run
our talons through and then be gone. Your white,
airy wings flutter with mine, beating thighs,
hips, breasts. We glide and climb.

Earlier,
before I loved you, when you and I were
monsters only, we wanted most to take
wing and be seen as floating mountains,
as harbingers, grand monstrous reckonings
while yet laying worldly claims, claims so deep

that our wide spanning wings left bodies bruised,
senses braised from our awesome calls and cries.

Soon, though, the tellers will wrap their tales round
the history of our talons as symbols,
as logic, speech, as metaphor released,
that dread tumble from bright, billowy clouds,
tomorrows, end on end, to our once and was
the unsown promise of feck and fallow ground.

L.B. Sedlacek

Physics and Mechanics

Lie in skin
does it fit
just right and
how does it
feel tight loose
do you like
the color the
smoothness the way
it lays across
the bones do
you like the
way it feels
when someone else
touches it or
you nick it
or cut it
or turn it
every which way
and can you
keep it clean
free of toxins
chemicals or burns
words and actions
so you can
trade it in

get credit for
repairs or just
wear it as
long as it
belongs to you.

Sergio Ortiz

Application for Canonization

I hereby request to be canonized
in the Holy Church of Love.

A man swore eternal love,
but his love was hell on earth.
I have more stigmata on my body
than those required by your Church,
greater tears than those expressed in cubic centimeters
by any of the aspirants to be consecrated,
greater number of hours of insomnia,
& on my knees so many eloquent calluses
that my friends call me:
Adela the genuflect.

One night
he made me walk like a bitch,
meow like a cat,
cry like a teenage girl
and sing like an old woman.

Another night
he forced me to kiss the portrait of his beloved.
I thought that maybe
he forced his beloved to kiss mine.
That same night —you do not know

how sorry I am to write this,

he screamed & called me a degenerate whore.

As for the requirement demanded by the Church:
You will love even if they grind you with rocks,
I can assure you that my love is immeasurable.
That man is my Greatest Good.

So, having been humiliated,
offended, vilified, set aside, & vexed;
having been confined to that strange latitude
which is: dead in life.

I, Adela Sobá, in full measure of my mental faculties,
humbly ask to be canonized as a lay saint
with the right to appear on the altars of horror.

An Animal Resembling Desire

Under an undecided bird
the day whines about orphanhoods,
clouds of absence hurt
a dark, putrid silence.

One by one the city awakens
its dead under a tired sky
to offer the waters
of its most recent words.

An animal resembling desire
extends laborious wings to petrify
the only tree standing.
Under fear's silhouette

infancy picks up its waist
and places it on a stone blind wall.
Under desperation leaves
a god made of solitudes

forces the clouds
to rain punishments
and transform boulders
into jaguars.

The Last Threshold

The promise to return
to the place where life began

Failure, to be banished
from an endless happiness

Shadows that wandered
the desert carrying their own past

A leaf-storm-fear
thrown to the felines of night

A beggar's desire going door
to door and sitting on the steps

of the last threshold
to discuss his ragged loneliness

his bones, a premonition
of the mirror where death calls

The indelible imprint of pain
and undaunted scars

A history of humiliating executioners
and false fabulists

The unsatisfied thirst of gods
who bully us with their vengeance

and a tree who in its old age
only nests birds of prey

Fred LaManna

A Sonnet to the Siren Aksinya

Dark eyeglasses,
bare shoulders, very unfriendly

Akaky Akakievich

Dashing through the waywards ways of how one should stay to
Attach with the golden enterprise of the sauntering side of thus
We have missed her while it is still of some esteem to plead over
The nasty but concurrent has been here to faithfully ponder the rue
Of a moreover steadfast caved in is the luminous sounds to not cuss
Overlapping was the needled and not so much of a torrid vapid clover

Here she was at the realm of the eased and not so much is there a bit
Ventilated spiral made from such bareness where one could have skin
That lacks the purpose of what can be the modern enough sharper claw
Was this a fearful moderate flight that handles a rueful missed from it
Can there not be a thumping over the leaking eyeglasses have been thin
It was all under the moderate fuss from who should dampen the true flaw

A Sonnet to the Siren Lorathi

Smoking cigarettes, small hands, peculiar

Akaky Akakievich

Sweetly effeminate was the shadow of the listless side to pounce
Upon the truly one must hamper the side of the victimless confound
Must be the loophole to restrain that many more of her gallant slaves
Was a fierce element to pretend to be all of the needy side of the trounce
Would we have to get away with the torrid challenge is a flatter resound
After what can be the mild faked out and tremendous were the waves

There to compete like a silky sort of meek trader was the hideous side
Of her constant puffing with the exhaled and taken to engulf the breeze
Was there not another stuffy mannerism to realize the franker paradise
Has given over to her responding gloved hands have trusted the true tide
With the boaty configured to result in muddied forms from the other seize
Must she have to gather the weakened pushy armaments to go chastise

A Sonnet to the Siren Davida

Dirty feet, long skirt, very cold hearted

Akaky Akakievich

Patient conditions have reveled in the same punishment around which
One has taken on the crusty but pointed sides to the careening spotty
Spots are here way to envision the mealy but protested about is there
ah
Find where she can dispose of the heady fervent not too challenged
witch
Was her side of the remaining tongueless perhaps there was not chatty
To humiliate there the modest taken aside is the handsome grainy blah

Thereafter bemused with the sheer convenience where one was up
front
To the whistling grind was the lackluster truly taken up by a vertical
stall
Here was her tempered and truly revered is the moreover not stood too
near
The reaping was ahead of the coldest moderate so much around the
blunt
Of each distance was how she walked with the middle side the nearly
tall
Could not evaporate into the meekest but not so promised to unshoe a
leer

Alex Hoffman-Ellis

How To Punish A Double Parker

Your brother's disheveled appearance
caroms off of lemonade-yellow walls the color of
madness, buzzing humming
like the final buzzer of a basketball game
that never stops
droning in the background
of crazies and orderlies
                (which is a matter of perspective in itself)
every time you visit your brother
on the sixth floor
his fat fingers flinging saucy sushi
steadily down his gullet
breath heavy as a steamship
his championship belt
of belly flesh falling and rising
between loudspeaker voices
and carts of flashy blinding
shiny insanity-white laundry

a man sits
his asscrack
that stupid fucking
gashy crack of ass
pouring out of his jeans
below his shrivelly-shrunken shirt

bleeding into frame
like LA drivers
carelessly careening
intersecting across cross-traffic

as your brother preaches Jesus praise
through noisy chews and chomps of shrimp
his toenails broken-glass jagged
and yellow
madness yellow like those 6th floors walls
that neon-light humhumming
and this man's stupid asshole staring me in the face
and all I can think about
is what I'm gonna do
if my neighbor double parks his car
in front of my family's house
one more time

Farmer's Market

The rising sun surges earthward
its rays violently highlighting
her gold-rimmed teeth
as she flings and massages
melodic sentences, Colombian Spanish
directed to the back where the other ladies stand
mahogany-toned hands well-worn
from an immeasurable time
spent in the confines
of her mother's kitchen
flipping scraping pounding rolling
molding shaping laboring
over 212 degree water and crackling oil
erupting from rusted skillets
like miniature supernovas

sweat beads bloom beneath dark brown eyes
time stands still yet whooshes by
she huddles over heavily used pans
flicking and nurturing gold-tinged pupusas
underneath the golden glow of sun
reflecting off her   gold-rimmed teeth
her half-smile   hardened, betraying a bullet
riddled husband and a paint-splotch stomach scar
serving as a grave marker
for the unborn son
they would never meet

Richard King Perkins II

Celestial Whip

The others are intimidated
by your tragic attitude—

the wires of your binding,
the ligature marks
of inward glories.

Across your body
I see jagged question marks—

records of your beating heart

the tiniest moments
of life and death.

It seems to me your years
as a street artist
are coming to an end

and now you'll specialize
in an apostasy
of plain white chairs and pain.

I'm not sure if these gripping hands
are the basis or the end-result

of loving you

but I do know

this is the only chance I'll have
to experience
your celestial whip

on the way to a heaven

I can never attend.

Gemini Mirror

We met beneath the humblest moon
as mist rolled down a deeper blue.

You told me how you kept a suitcase
packed in every room

filled with things forgotten
and overlooked

and that we'd never have any children
because you could only deliver pain.

For the last five years
you've stared into a gemini mirror

while licking
your dirty thoughts clean

and offering
to do the same for me.

Because I don't know where you come from
I ask which star is yours—

your hand sweeps
the fullest arcing frontier

indicating everywhere

and all.

Gelatin Plateaus

You're scared to exchange words
fearing that I'll intersperse my voice

with a disastrous elixir
designed to make you love me.

In my guise as a simple hitchhiker
with a broken guitar

you've driven past
at least a dozen times

coursing the roundabout
with your left foot tapping out the window.

Cast from the joke of a raven
you dance naked but impenetrable

in a tongueless world of gelatin plateaus
and abalone snow.

The sound you're hearing in your mind
is only a mortar and pestle—

the killing powder was consumed
when you first imagined

the swollenness
of my lips around your nipple;

felt the insistence of glacial stone
opening furrows of ochre and loam.

Caitlin Thomson

The Yard

There is an Azalea bush in the front yard that our friend
once referred to as the pride of the neighborhood.
I was not sure if she was seeing it as it is, untrimmed
branches, dead growth, or as it once was, orange flowers
from soil to air, singing all sorts of glory.
I am more interested in the raspberry bushes that line
the back fence, nothing to look at, everything to taste.

Norman Klein

White

All milk, cottage cheese, and snowy owls.
Most sheets, sinks, lab rats, paper towels,
sailor hats, and all small and harmless lies.

Towering flowering ash trees. July night
firefly light winking in a child's eye.
Some peonies, and Arabian show horses,

silk sails, chess pieces, and the neck stripe
of a killdeer, the belly and chest of a booby.
Baby teeth, and taller peaks in the Pyrenees.

All kinds of things are half or mostly,
and lest we forget there is also
Snow, Barry, and Betty.

Reality Times 3

We begin with three men, Bob, Bill, and Hal, who are different sizes but each is appealing and attractive in his own way. They have a little wear on them. They could be anywhere from 38 to 48.

Same for the women: Meg, Jan, and Ava are different sizes, but each is appealing and attractive in her own way. Same age range and all three wear clothes that fit, and like the men they are not currently in a serious relationship. Oh, by the way, only first names will be used. We don't want real names, for dozens of reasons.

Here is the concept: each man will date each woman, and on each date the men and women will score each other. Each man and each woman will have 33 points to give on each of the three dates, and each date will be filmed. There is also one rule that must be obeyed. No player may reveal the points he or she gave, or intends to give. Anyone caught doing this will have all of their points erased.

The highest scoring man and woman will receive two hundred dollars for each point they earned on the three dates. At the end of the show, the winning man will be asked who he thinks the winning woman is. If he is right his winnings are doubled. Then the winning woman does the same thing.

The first date will be a long visit to the zoo, or a museum, or Aquarium, and the daters get to choose.

The second date is a long walk on a beach or through a park, followed by dinner at a restaurant. If it's raining they can do something inside.

See a movie, go to a mall, take a tour … whatever.

The third date begins with dinner, then the daters retire to the honeymoon suite of a luxury hotel and watch a favorite movie together, or go to a movie or club. They can also spend the night together or not.

That's it. It can't miss. It's foolproof. Self-correcting. Sponsors will love it. After two months of testing we found one possible glitch, but it turned out to be nothing. It was self-correcting. One idiot asked woman 1 and 2 for follow-on secret dates right after the show dates thinking he could be extra charming and wonderful with no cameras on him, but both of the women saw through his scheme and gave men 2 and 3 higher points than the idiot.

But what if Bob happens to meet Jan on the street. Don't worry sponsors, don't worry, America, it's in his and her contract. All they can do is wave. Or what if Bob is in a parking lot and notices that Jan is following him in her car. He stops his car and tries to get her plate number but she speeds off before he can. His first thought is to turn her in. In real life grandmothers do that, but what if Bob turns around and follows her and she lets him catch her, and they go to a motel. Who cares? We call what's going on reality, but it's love that makes the show, and the fourth show in the series has to be the best show, because all six people will be on stage telling secrets, and asking each other what they were really thinking on this day or that, and the funniest, wildest, sexiest person gets a bonus check of ten thousand dollars. But, what if two people say they are going to get married. Do they get two checks? No. Because when they say it, the audience will go wild for ten seconds, and that will be the end of it.

www.ingramcontent.com/pod-product-compliance
Lightning Source LLC
Chambersburg PA
CBHW030436010526
44118CB00011B/656